1000 PLUS
Household Hints

1000 PLUS Household Hints

On Kitchen, Beauty, Garden, Interiors,
Cooking, Health, Hygiene, Clothes,
First-aid, Jewellery & many more

Tanushree Podder

PUSTAK MAHAL®
Delhi•Mumbai•Patna•Hyderabad•Bangalore

Publishers
Pustak Mahal, Delhi-110006

Sales Centres
- 6686, Khari Baoli, Delhi-110006, *Ph:* 3944314, 3911979
- 10-B, Netaji Subhash Marg, Daryaganj, New Delhi-110002
  Ph: 3268292, 3268293, 3279900 • *Fax:* 011-3280567

Administrative Office
J-3/16 (Opp. Happy School), Daryaganj, New Delhi-110002
Ph: 3276539, 3272783, 3272784 • *Fax:* 011-3260518
E-mail: pustakmahal@vsnl.com • *Website:* www.pustakmahal.com

Branch Offices
BANGALORE : 22/2, Mission Road (Shama Rao's Compound), Bangalore-560027
Ph: 2234025 • *Fax:* 080-2240209 • *E-mail:* rapidexblr@satyam.net.in

MUMBAI : 23-25 , Zaoba Wadi (Opp. VIP Showroom), Thakurdwar,
Mumbai-400002, *Ph:* 2010941 • *Fax:* 022-2053387
E-mail: rapidex@bom5.vsnl.net.in

PATNA : Khemka House, Ist Floor (Opp. Women's Hospital),
Ashok Rajpath, Patna-800004, *Telefax:* 0612-673644

HYDERABAD : 5-1-707/1, Brij Bhawan, Bank Street, Koti, Hyderabad-500095
Ph: 4737530 • *Fax:* 040-4737290

© **Pustak Mahal,** 6686 Khari Baoli, Delhi-110006

ISBN 81-223-0013-8

Fully Revised : March, 2002

Printed at : Kwality Offset Printing Press
Naraina, New Delhi – Ph : 5698469

Publisher's Note

Management has pervaded every sphere of modern life, so how could the home front remain exempt from its purview? Every homemaker is a manager irrespective of whether the setting is rural or urban. She manages to perform the household chores with such clinical efficiency that it seems to be a very easy job. But a little insight into the daily chores of a homemaker would reveal the enormity of the task. One cannot but appreciate the meticulous planning which goes behind the smooth functioning of a home. Inspite of so many modern gadgets meant for easing the task, the onus still rests on the homemaker to streamline all activities so that the home front rolls on well oiled wheels, smoothly and efficiently.

Pustak Mahal, in keeping up with its tradition, has been making great endeavour to publish 'House-keeping series' to lessen the burden of the Indian women. This book, **Over 1000 Household Hints,** is one such effort in that direction. The underlying principle of the book, written in a simple language, is to help young women with the innumerable problems which she faces when she first sets up her home. This book becomes all the more relevant to the working women who don't have the required time to learn through the 'trial and error' method.

It is hoped that the book will prove useful and worth preserving.

—Publishers

Contents

Introduction

Many books are written on different subjects but not many books have been written on solutions to the common problems faced by a young home-maker when she first sets up her home. The young woman is totally nonplussed about the myriad little problems that crop up every day. How to store the greens in the fridge, how to turn out soft *'chapatis'* which will be appreciated by her husband, and how to make the resources last a little longer?

As a young bride, I faced a lot of problems and did not know where to look for the answers. Since I had always been a tomboy who had no interest in entering the kitchen or doing any household work, I was totally clueless about running the house. And when I faced the problems, I would sit and cry because I did not know how to deal with them. I would spend hours trying to prepare a dish, as given in a recipe book and land up with an inedible stuff just because I had put some extra teaspoons of salt in it. In my endeavour to become a perfect cook and a housekeeper, I pored over many books, contacted many people and maintained a diary with all the tips and hints given to me by my mother, aunts and grandmother. Those were hard times and I learnt it the hard way. I must have wasted a lot, thrown a lot, to learn my lessons. It was a perfect case of learning through 'trial and error'. It took me years to learn all the tricks and yet I am far from being perfect. And then I realised that there must be hundreds of young women, like me, who do not have the patience and the opportunity to learn through advice or 'trial and error'.

The book becomes more relevant in the present era because most young women are working and have neither the time nor the opportunity to go around, hunting for hints and making notes of them. They have to learn through trial and error method of learning. This method can be pretty time consuming and one incurs a lot of wastage, too. And wastage in the modern times will just not do.

This book has taken many years to be compiled. I wanted my daughters to have an easier time than me, when they grow up and take to home making. This book took shape when I dreamt of handing over the thousands of hints collected by me, over the years, to my daughters and the other young girls of this country. I hope this book comes handy for all those who are struggling to cope with the sudden demands made on them.

Although a lot of care has been taken while compiling the ideas and tips into neat sections, there may be certain areas, which are not clearly demarcated, mainly because the matter is common to two or more situations.

I think that the introduction cannot be complete unless I thank all the people who have been involved with me in bringing out this book. Bringing out a book requires a lot of effort and this book has been created solely by the united efforts of my family. A large and heartfelt chunk of thanks goes to my husband and my daughters who have made their precious time available for the book. They have come up with very constructive ideas and helped me with the editing. I would like to thank my husband, especially, since he has been with me through the birth pangs of this book. He has held my hand when I despaired, given me the moral courage when I felt like giving it up, supported me when I faltered and made himself available when I needed his presence.

—Tanushree Podder

Kitchen

Kitchen

The most expensive commodity in today's world is time. Gone are the days when women worked in the kitchen and spent their entire time planning the meals and sweating over their stoves. In the fast moving world that has no place for wastage of time or money, it is necessary that people make the best of their resources.

Apart from the time factor, there is a lot of wisdom required in maintaining the family budget within the available resources. This requires good planning and knowledge of cutting corners wherever possible. Economizing is an essential factor for the homemaker. In the coming millennium, it would be imperative for everyone to become more prudent and avoid wastage of every kind. Be it the energy resources, the food material or the natural products, conservation will be the key to survival.

Kitchen is one place where health becomes the casualty when one panders to the taste buds. It is also the place where a balanced diet and common sense play a very important role. There are hundreds of tried and tested methods to save time, fuel, and money. These methods have been discovered by wise women who knew where their priorities lay. By sharing the valuable tips with the others, they have done a good turn to the society.

The kitchen tips are divided into several parts, cooking tips, cleaning tips, economy tips, storing tips, gadget tips, anti-pest tips and practical tips. ·

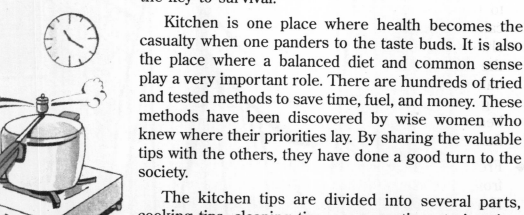

COOKING TIPS

Cooking can be a pleasure for some but a painful experience for many modern women. With lesser time at hand, she is always in search of short cuts and substitute methods. For the inexperienced cook, an excess of salt or burnt rice can become an embarrassing experience. It is at times like this, one wishes for tips that could take care of the problems. Here are some very valuable tips to help the harassed homemaker.

Of Cakes and Cookies

◆ Are you one of those cooks who despair over their cakes, which fall flat and refuse to rise? There is no need to lose hope. Try this tip for a deliciously soft and spongy cake - add 2 tablespoons of any aerated cola to the cake batter for a delicious cake.

◆ And just in case you happen to be a vegetarian who refuses to use eggs but likes to bake a cake, here is a tip for you. To make an eggless cake spongier, add the juice of 1 lime to the batter just before pouring the batter into the baking tray.

◆ With the jet set age, most of us do not have the time to bake a leisurely cake, yet we like to have our cake and eat it too. If you are one of those who are always rushing about, there is no need to go into the long rituals of mixing the batter. If you want to bake a cake in a hurry, just mix all the ingredients together with a level tablespoon of limejuice. No beating is required. The cake will be as good and fluffy as when you beat it well.

◆ From cakes to pancakes is nothing like being thrown from the pan into the fire. It is quite a simple process. Here is a tip to help you along. While making pancakes, pour the batter from a jug instead of ladling, for an easy and even spread.

◆ To make professional looking chocolate leaves, to decorate your cake, just melt a little milk chocolate in a bowl over a double boiler. Using a small brush, smear the chocolate on the dull side of fresh, clean rose leaves. Leave in a cool place to harden and then carefully peel away the real leaf.

◆ If you cannot get perfect chocolate curls to use on your dessert, or the cheese curls to go with your pizzas, just use your potato peeler to grate cheese or chocolates for making chocolate curls.

◆ Sometimes, we land up with a cake batter that is as thick as a cement mix. Thick batter does not result in soft cakes. To thin the batter, use water instead of milk. The cake will turn out much softer than you expected. (See Annexure-1)

◆ If you are one of those who thought glycerine is only for softening the skin, think again. A teaspoon of glycerine added to the cake batter can give you a spongy and soft cake, too.

◆ Professional cake makers swear by this secret tip. Try adding a little lemon juice to your cake batter, the next time. You will be surprised at the light and spongy effect.

◆ The soda water has many qualities. It can help you make a lovely, light pastry. Just use soda water instead of tap water for kneading the dough.

◆ Those cake lovers, who have yet to buy their first oven, can still bake their cakes and enjoy the same. To bake a cake without an oven, use your *'roti tava'* on which the cake dish can be placed. Cover it with a lid and turn the gas on slow for the same period of time as you would, an oven.

Eggy Tips

◆ Are you envious of the tastier and fluffier omelette made by your friend? You can make an equally good one by adding a little gram flour while beating the eggs.

◆ If you are unable to make a poached egg to perfection and have the white spreading all over your pan, try this tip. Add a few drops of limejuice or vinegar to the water to prevent the whites from spreading and watch the look of wonder on the faces around you.

◆ Most of us love the delicious drink called 'eggnog' but have to wait for someone to make it for us. Making it is quite simple, really. Beat one egg thoroughly. To this, add a cup of milk and grated nutmeg, vanilla essence or brandy. Stir it up well and your drink is ready.

◆ Adding 1-tablespoon water to the egg before beating it will also result in a much larger and fluffier omelette.

◆ Most of us hate the sight of the black colour on the yolks of our boiled eggs. To prevent the discolouration of the egg yolk in boiled eggs, immerse them in cold water immediately after removing them from hot water.

◆ What happens when you want to boil the eggs and land up with a cracked one? You have two options, bear with a boiled egg with its white spilled into the water or try this tip - add a teaspoon of vinegar to the water in which you want to boil the egg. You will manage to get a perfectly boiled egg.

◆ I always found it difficult to take the fried eggs out of the pan. They would disintegrate and run all over the pan. This happened till I found the solution to the problem. While frying eggs, adding a little vinegar and salt to the ghee helps in quickening the coagulation and prevents disintegration, too.

- For a delicious dish of scrambled eggs, use a dollop of cottage cheese instead of the usual milk and butter.

- To make a soft and fluffy omelette, heat a non-stick pan and add a little more butter than usual. Now beat the egg and stir briskly (even while frying) with a fork. This way, more air goes in your omelette, making it light and fluffy. Fry till done and serve hot.

Jams, Ice Creams and Desserts

- Have you ever wondered why the branded jams have a nice and delicious flavour? While the home made ones are not quite so good. Add a couple of lemon peels and simmer for 5 minutes and then compare the two. You will not be disappointed.

- Making jams and marmalades at home can be economical and you can be assured of genuine ingredients. If you use sugar made from sugarcane rather than sugar beet it will give you a better set and more jam.

- Sometimes preparing a new type of dessert can become a real problem, especially if you do not have time to spend in the kitchen. Here is a recipe for a quick and novel dessert. When jelly is almost set, churn it lightly with a little fresh cream in a mixer and let it set again. A fluffy and unusual sweet dish is ready for the children.

- Children love anything that has a little fizz in it. The ordinary jelly can be made to fizz with a littler improvisation. To make fizzy jellies, heat only a little quantity of water to melt the jelly crystals. For the remaining quantity, substitute water with sparkling wine, ginger ale or lemonade.

- Come summertime and everyone is ready for the ice cream. But they do not want the homemade ones because they are not as good as the one available in the parlours. Don't despair if the family rejects your efforts. Next time; try this hint for soft, home made ice creams. Add stiffly beaten white of an egg to the thickened milk, just before removing it from the heat and stir well.

◆ One of the problems we face while making ice creams is the formation of crystals in them. To make crystal free and creamier ice creams, use creamless milk or fresh milk. Add the cream later, while churning the mixer.

◆ For an added crunch and taste, sprinkle leftover biscuit or cake crumbs over vanilla ice cream. Children love its delicious taste.

◆ Caramel puddings are a perennial favorite of most families. Sometimes, however, the pudding becomes a little soft and doesn't set so well. There is an easy solution to combat this problem. While making caramel pudding, mix some custard powder to the egg-milk mixture. The pudding will be firmer and tastier.

◆ Honey is not just for the bees. It can be used for various desserts and drinks. It is light and nutritious besides containing several healthy elements. To get tastier custard, add a little honey along with the sugar.

◆ For those of you who love Indian desserts but find it a little difficult to cope with the complexities of making one, here is a simple tip. Making *'moong dal'* or *'urad dal halwa'* becomes very easy if you add 1 teaspoon of wheat flour to the heated ghee before adding the *'dal'* paste. It will not stick to the frying pan at all.

◆ Come festival time and we are inundated with the lot of sweets brought by well-wishers, friends and relatives. If the sweets are not consumed within a couple of days, they harden up in the fridge. Hard and stale *'pedas'* and *' burfees'* can be used to make fresh sweets. Mash them and put them in a heavy

CASHEW NUT

bottom pan along with a little milk and grated coconut. Keep stirring on low heat till the mixture leaves the sides of the pan. Pour in a greased plate and cut into pieces.

◆ For delicious *shrikhand,* place the curd in a small-perforated vessel covered with a muslin cloth. Place this in a larger vessel to collect the drained water. Keep both these vessels in the fridge, overnight. Powder sugar and a few cardamoms and mix with thickened curd. Garnish with a handful of chopped cashewnuts and almonds.

◆ If you have been wondering about the size and softness of the *'gulab jamuns'* sold at the shops, you can make an equally good one at home. While making *'gulab jamuns',* put a cashew nut inside each one while shaping them. They will look bigger and taste better.

◆ If you want to whip up a quick dessert, which is both nutritious and delicious, try this. To make tasty banana bread in a jiffy, beat 250 gm flour, 250 gm sugar, 60 ml oil, 3 bananas and $1^1/_2$ teaspoon of baking powder and bake till done.

◆ If homemade *gulab jamuns* have not turned out soft and fluffy, steam them in a pressure cooker (with the weight) along with the syrup for about ten minutes. Voila! You will be surprised at the softness when you bite into them.

◆ Most first timers have problems with their *'kheer'.* Either it turns out to be too thick or too thin. I remember making it the first time. It turned out so thick that I had to keep adding milk to get the right consistency and then I had to add sugar to make it sweet. Turning the thick *'kheer'* into an acceptable consistency is quite easy; one just adds a little more milk to it. And to thicken *'kheer',* you could add a little semolina roasted in ghee.

SEMOLINA ROASTED IN GHEE

MILK

THIN KHEER

THICK KHEER

◆ For a tasty dessert, boil 2 cups of milk with 3 teaspoon of sugar. Add small pieces of bread, a little butter, 2 beaten eggs and a few drops of vanilla essence. Mix well and bake for about 45 minutes.

◆ With the growing awareness about the ills of using too much *'ghee'*, one is hesitant while using the stuff. Wise people always have a solution; you could try it, too. While preparing *'burfees'* and *'laddoos'*, roast the gram flour in an oven. You will need less ghee and the sweets will taste better, too.

◆ If you are a health conscious person, make a health packed *'laddoo'* for the family. Mix *'ragi'* flour, gram flour, and wheat flour in the proportion of 2:1:1 and make *'laddoos'*. They are nutritious and children love the taste, too.

◆ For a special type of milkshake, take 3 tablespoons of any fruit jam, add a glass of milk and beat in a mixie. Chill and serve. It tastes delicious. I don't know so much about the adults but children definitely love all kinds of milk shake.

Fish and Chicken

◆ During my initial years in the kitchen, I tried to live with the broken and burnt pieces of fried fish. You need not suffer the embarrassment if you coat fish pieces with rice flour before frying. This trick will prevent them from sticking to the frying pan. (See Annexure-2)

◆ I also had to suffer the pain of burns after the ordeal of frying fish. It took me years to find a solution. Before frying fish, add a pinch of turmeric to the oil. This prevents the oil from spluttering out of the pan on to your hands.

◆ How often have you cooked the meat for hours and discovered it to be tough. The trick is to make it tender. One or two pieces of betel nut or unripe papaya are excellent meat tenderizers.

PAPAYA ⚬ ⚬ BETEL NUT

◆ Homemade chicken *tikkas* can sometimes land up being as hard as pebbles. For delicious and extra soft chicken *tikka,* mix one egg into the marinade.

◆ With Chinese dishes becoming an all time favourite, one can never learn enough about perfecting them. If you want the balls of chicken to be crisp and tasty while making chicken or vegetarian Manchurian, add a little rice flour to the mixture before frying. The balls will be crisper.

◆ Here is another tip to cook meat to perfection without fretting for hours. To tenderize meat and add flavour to it, marinate it for an hour in beer.

◆ What does one do when the chicken gravy becomes too watery and you have guests coming for dinner? Well! Just add breadcrumbs and 1-2 teaspoon *garam masala* powder to the chicken gravy. And hey, presto! A nice and thick gravy is ready.

◆ To make a quick sauce for boiled chicken or fish when unexpected guests arrive, stir 2 teaspoon of curry powder into 1-cup curd and add a little salt. Heat to serving temperature and spoon over each serving. You will have the guests eating out of your hand.

Paneer and Cheese

◆ Cooking paneer can be quite a pain. How else does one explain the tough and hard pieces one finds in the paneer curries. They can, however, be softened up, easily. While frying *'paneer',* add a little salt to the oil for even browning and dip the *'paneer'* cubes in hot water so that they remain soft. (See Annexure-1)

◆ To make use of spilt milk, make some *'paneer'.* To spilt milk, add sour curd and obtain soft *'paneer'.*

◆ There is another method to make the *'paneer'* soft. Dip *'paneer'* in salt water before adding to any curry, this will make them softer.

◆ For *paneer* curry, add a little grated *paneer* to make it thick and delicious.

Breads — Indian and Exotic

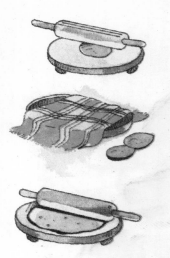

◆ Many of my friends from the South of India wonder how their counterparts in the North manage to get such soft *'chapatis'*. It is quite simple; just add 2-3 tablespoon homemade *'paneer'* and milk to wheat flour. You will get soft, smooth and nutritious dough for *'chapatis'*.

◆ If you are one of the adventurous types of cooks, try this recipe for a variation. For making soft *'puris'* and *'chapatis',* add a mashed and boiled potato while mixing the dough. (See Annexure-7)

◆ To make *'rotis'* and *'parathas'* soft, use warm water while kneading the dough.

◆ To make *'methi parathas'* tastier, add a little gramflour to the wheat flour and knead the dough with a little sour curd.

◆ If you are stuck with leftover *'chapatis'* or *'parathas',* don't throw them away. Wrap them in a clean cloth and pack into an airtight container that fits into the cooker and cook for 2 whistles. They will become hot and soft, once again.

◆ If your *'puris'* do not turn out as fluffy and nice, as you would like them to be, try this one. Add a little milk while mixing the dough.

◆ For nice and crisp *'puris',* heat some oil till it smokes; add this to the *maida* while making the dough.

◆ If you like your *'puris'* crisp, while kneading dough for *'puris',* add a little rice flour to the wheat flour.

◆ For nutritious and colourful *'parathas',* knead the dough with spinach puree or beetroot juice. The colours will lure the kids into having an extra serving.

◆ The softness of *'bhaturas'* depends on the extent of fermentation. Crumble 1-2 slices of bread and add to the *'bhatura'* batter for quick fermentation.

◆ To roll out a perfect *'bhatura',* roll out small portions of the dough into small *'puris'* and cover them with a damp cloth. Roll them out just before frying.

Mushy Mushrooms and Vegetables

◆ Mushrooms often become dark and discoloured while cooking. To prevent them from doing so, dip mushrooms in warm water to which a tablespoon of milk has been added. (See Annexure-3)

◆ I love eating mushrooms but I couldn't cook them because they always broke when I cooked them. Only recently, a friend told me to add a teaspoon of lemon juice to the butter while frying mushrooms. This prevents them from breaking.

◆ Often one is hounded with the sticky lot of ladyfingers while frying. This ruins the dish. To ensure that ladyfingers don't turn black or stick to the vessel while cooking, add a spoonful of curd to them.

◆ Foxed by the half roasted brinjal? After roasting a brinjal for *'bharta',* place it in a plate and cover it with a lid. Any raw portion that remains will also get cooked. The latent heat trapped within the lid will do your work for you.

◆ Here is another tip on *'bhartas'*. For a *'baigan bharta'* with a difference, add a little green masala and curd.

◆ I always wondered how the professional cooks managed to keep their spinach so green or the cauliflower so white, till I learnt their trick. To retain the original colour of spinach, broccoli and cabbage, douse them in ice-cold water just after boiling them.

◆ Let us admit, we still nurture a fondness for the colour white, be it the skin or anything else. To retain the whiteness of potatoes while boiling, add a little lime juice and some sugar.

◆ If you add a pinch of alum to the potatoes while boiling, they will remain white.

◆ Most Indians like their curries to look rich and red. To give your curry a nice and red colour, de-seed two red chillies and soak them in water. When the chillies become soft, crush them and add the water to the gravy.

◆ Let us face it; colours do play a very important part in cooking. Peas don't look half as good, if they do not have a garden fresh green colour. While using green peas in *'pulao'*, apply a little oil to them so that they retain their original colour.

◆ For garnishing *pulaos*, fry onions with a pinch of sugar. They will turn brown faster and impart a nice colour to the *pulao*, too.

◆ Using the right substitute is an art by itself. If you run out of breadcrumbs while making cutlets, use crushed cornflakes or sieved semolina and they will be equally crisp.

◆ Frying onions is a chore I detest. One can go on and on, trying to fry them to the right degree. But I have learnt a trick. Add a pinch of salt to the chopped onions while frying them for seasoning. They will turn soft quicker.

◆ While on frying onions, I must share a tip for those who want to use very little oil and manage to burn their onions. Adding a little milk to the onions while frying will give them a rich colour and prevent burning.

◆ I never remember to soak the *'Rajmah'*,*'chana'* etc., the previous night and so I can never get down to cooking these pulses. But, now I have discovered a method, which eliminates the problem. When you have to cook pulses like *'chana'* etc. and have forgotten to soak them overnight, don't panic. Just put the chana in a flask full of boiling water for an hour. They will be ready for cooking within no time.

◆ Germinated legumes can be a very healthy addiction. A friend of mine always adds dried and powdered germinated legumes to baby food to improve the nutritive value. Needless to say, her baby wins all the 'healthy baby' contests.

◆ Many Indian recipes, especially the ones from Maharashtra and down South, require roasted groundnuts. To get perfectly roasted groundnuts, sprinkle a little water over them to prevent the nuts from getting burnt. They will become crisper and the skin will come off easily.

- Before roasting brinjals for making *'baingan bharta'*, smear them with mustard oil. The skin will peel off easily.

- For the novice cook who always misjudges the water used for the gravies and finds the resultant gravy quite a thin one, here is a very helpful tip. Roast groundnuts and sesame seeds and powder them. This powder can be used to thicken gravies as well as to add a delicious flavour to the curry.

- If you are fed up of the soggy taste of your *bhindi fry'*, just add a few drops of lemon juice to the ladyfingers while cooking them. You will love the crispy taste.

- Most mothers have a problem with their children as far as bitter-gourd is concerned. Yet, it is one of the vegetables that we want our children to eat. What you can do to remove the bitterness is to soak the bitter gourd pieces in curd, overnight. In the morning you can either stuff them or cook them in any other method. Children will not complain about the bitterness.

- To add a fresh taste to leftover gravies, roast and grind cumin seeds and store in a bottle. Add a pinch in gravies and *'raitas'* to get a deliciously fresh flavour.

- This tip is for those who can never decide the amount of salt to add to the *'sambar,'* and land up adding a little more to be on the safe side. To remove excess salt from *'sambar'*, soup or gravy, add a bowl of cooked rice.

- Using leftover stuff is a big challenge. Each time I make *'dosas',* I am left with a substantial amount of the coconut chutney. I always fretted over the wastage till a friend taught me the trick of using the leftover chutney. It can be used to make a delicious dish. Add cooked potatoes, beans, green peas and a spoonful of coconut oil for flavour and boil for 5 minutes. Garnish with coriander leaves. The resulting vegetable korma can be served with hot chapattis.

Chutneys and Pickles

◆ Talking of chutneys, here is a recipe to make a tasty chutney, in a jiffy. Grind 2 cucumbers, 1 tomato, a few cumin seeds, and ginger and green chilli. Add salt and lime juice to taste. This chutney can be served with all sorts of stuffed *'parathas'* and snacks.

◆ Instead of adding curd to green chutney, try adding limejuice. The chutney will not only be tastier; it will remain fresh for a longer time and will also retain its healthy green colour.

◆ If the tamarind chutney turns out too watery, just add a little *'amchur'* to thicken it.

◆ For a delicious, instant chutney, mix one teaspoon of 'amchur' powder with $1/4$ teaspoon of cumin powder, 3 teaspoons of sugar, $1/2$ cup water and boil for 2-3 minutes on low heat.

◆ A pickle out of orange peels? No, I am not joking. Cut orange peel into small pieces. Heat a little oil in a pan. Add mustard seeds. When they crackle, add the peels and sauté them for 5 minutes. Add tamarind pulp and salt; cook till it dries up. Keep aside. Crumble jaggery in a separate vessel; add the orange peel and mix. Spice it up with chilli powder and turmeric powder and cool for 2 minutes to get a delicious pickle. Mango peels also can be used for similar pickle. But, remember to consume it within a couple of days and don't forget to keep the bottle in the fridge.

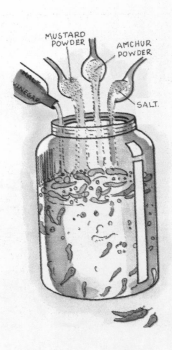

◆ Slit green chillies into halves, put them in a glass jar. Add enough malt vinegar, 1-teaspoon salt, 1-teaspoon *'amchur'* powder, and 1 teaspoon mustard powder. Mix well, cover the bottle with a small muslin cloth and keep in the sun for 2 days. A delicious chilli pickle will be ready.

◆ For a healthy, tasty and oil- free pickle, chop green chillies and ginger into small pieces and store them in a bottle of salted limejuice. Refrigerate it after a few days. This pickle will keep for a long time.

Papads

◆ Crisp *'papads'*, an all time favourite but they also absorb a lot of oil while frying. Roasting the *'papads'* in a toaster is healthier. You will get crisp papads without the calories.

◆ For those of you who can't have their *'papads'* without the touch of oil in them, here is a tip. Instead of deep-frying *'papads'*, smear oil on both the sides of it and roast on the gas. They not only taste better but save on oil, too.

◆ If there can be variations in the recipes of omelettes, why not in the ones for *'uthappams'*? For tastier *'uthappams'*, add finely chopped mushrooms or cottage cheese to the batter.

Koftas and Cutlets

◆ For years I continued to be foxed about the hard *'koftas'* that defied all remedies. But you can definitely avoid making the mistake. For softer and tastier *'koftas'*, just add 1 teaspoon of baking powder to the dough.

◆ While making crisp banana and potato wafers, sprinkle salt water on the cut chips, for better taste and texture.

◆ If you have run out of chilli sauce for your Chinese dishes, take a little chilli pickle and grind to a paste. This will make a good substitute.

◆ To get a new taste in the same old vegetables, add a teaspoon of any pickle to the onions being fried in the oil along with the other ingredients.

◆ For tasty cutlets from leftover vegetables, boil, peel and mash potatoes with salt, chopped green chillies, coriander leaves and ginger—garlic paste. Mix with the leftover vegetables. Take small portions, roll into round balls, flatten and dip the balls in beaten egg. Roll in breadcrumbs and fry.

◆ To make potato *'kachoris'* crisp; add a little roasted gramflour to the mashed potatoes.

◆ Children are generally fascinated by a colourful spread on the dining table. To give them an eye-full, add 1 cup of grated carrot when you cook rice. The rice will be healthier, tasty and colourful.

◆ When you have a fussy child who doesn't like drinking milk. Mix 1-cup carrot juice with $1/_2$ litre milk. The milk will be tastier and have a beautiful colour, too.

◆ To increase the quantity of fresh cream, add $1/_2$ cup thick curd and $1/_2$ cup milk. Whip it up, nicely. This will not only double the quantity but taste better, too.

◆ The chill in the weather during the winters can pose while churning the butter. To make things easy, remember, butter can be churned in a jiffy during the winter, by pouring $1/_2$ cup of hot water into the jug or mixie in which you are whisking the cream. Swirl the water around so that the vessel warms up. Then add the cream to it and proceed as usual.

◆ For those of you who get foxed by certain ingredients mentioned in the recipe books, here is a tip. Self-raising flour can be made at home. To get self-raising flour, sieve each cup of 'maida' with $1^1/_2$ teaspoon baking powder and a pinch of salt.

Pakoras and Dahi Wadas

◆ Here is a word of advice for all those persons who love to eat *'pakoras'* but feel guilty about the amount of oil consumed during the binges. Add a pinch of salt to the oil while frying *'pakoras'* or *'koftas'* and you will be surprised to note how little oil is absorbed.

◆ Some people like their *'pakoras'* soft so the above tip is quite useless for them. For those who like it soft, add a pinch of baking powder along with 1-2 teaspoons of hot oil to the batter. (See Annexure-1)

PAKODAS WITH LESS OIL

- *'Pakoras'* will turn out crisper and tastier if you add a little cornflour to the gramflour while mixing the dough.

- Many of us turn out soggy onion *'pakoras'* and don't quite know what went wrong. The fact is that the batter, which is perfect, turns dilute when the onions are added because of the juice that the onions release. To make crisp onion *'pakoras'*, just sprinkle a little salt on the onions and mix well. Keep aside for a few minutes. Soon the onions will become moist. Mix in the gram flour and *masalas* and fry.

- Half the excitement in cooking is the presentation of a dish. For exciting shapes of *'papads'*, cut them with the scissors before frying or roasting. The children will lap them up in no time.

- Seasoning is another area where one can easily go wrong. Even after years of cooking, I sometimes land up with a salty soup. If you have added more salt to the *'dal'*, put a piece of potato or a lump of dough in it, to soak up the extra salt.

- While cooking leafy vegetables like spinach or cabbage, always add salt at the end, when it is almost cooked and the quantity has reduced.

- While making *'dahi wadas'*, add a little curd to the ground *'dal'* and mix well. The *'wadas'* will turn out softer and absorb less oil, too.

- To make the *'dahi wada'* softer and tastier, add one or two boiled and mashed potatoes in the *dal* paste.

- Dip bread slices in water, for a minute, squeeze them dry and crumble them. They can be added to the dough for *'urad dal wadas'*, if you need to increase the quantity instantly. They can also be added to potato filling, for *'alu parathas'*. If you dip the slices in milk instead of water, you can use them in *'paneer* or egg *bhurjee'*.

- If you have an adventurous palate and the penchant for trying out novel ideas, here's one for you. For an unusual taste and flavour in the soup, add a teaspoon of mint paste to the onion or tomato soup.

Miscellaneous

◆ The sight of dried up slices of bread is enough to take away the appetite. But what does one do with the dried up loaves? To freshen up the dried up bread, steam it for a couple of minutes. It will be as good and soft as a fresh one.

TIL OIL

SOFT IDLI

◆ The North Indian cooks are always mystified about the soft and delicious *'idlis'* made so easily, by the South Indian counterparts. The solution is quite simple. To get soft and spongy *'idlis',* add a little horse gram paste to the *'idli'* batter. Mix well and keep aside for an hour.

◆ For soft *'idlis',* add 2 teaspoons of *'til'* oil to the batter before you set it aside for fermentation.

◆ Grated carrots, cabbage, cauliflower and peas, if added to the *idli* batter make the *idlis* colourful, tasty and nutritious.

◆ If you are surprised by the arrival of unexpected guests at meal time, don't panic. It is easy enough to dish up quick curries. For quick cooking of gravy, use already fried onions, which have been refrigerated.

◆ Salad tastes best when it is fresh, crisp and cold. To keep the salad fresh, chill the serving bowl before serving the salad in it.

◆ To prepare a vegetable *biryani* or *korma*, with a meaty flavour, add a little lemon grass while cooking it.

KORMA OR BIRYANI

LEMON GRASS

◆ A dear friend of mine gave this tip, when my husband was posted at a remote place and I could not manage a maidservant. If you want to serve hot *'chapatis'* to your guests and have no help, half roast the *'chapatis'* and wrap in a clean napkin. After laying the table, bake them once again on the *'tawa'*. They will be hot and steaming in no time.

◆ Ever noticed the blackish colour in certain vegetables, which are rich in iron? To enhance the iron content in the dish, cook spinach, brinjal and fenugreek in an iron pan.

◆ For a high protein diet, mix soybean and wheat together in the ratio of 1: 9 and grind together. Use this flour for making *'chapatis'*. This is especially good during the winter months when the body needs more nourishment.

◆ While cooking pasta, noodles or macaroni, add a dash of yellow food colour to the water. This will give the pasta a buttery look.

◆ Most of the recipes give dressings, which are very high in fat contents. Try this for low calorie content. Mix some curd with honey to prepare an excellent dressing for chopped parsley, mint, onion and paprika. (See Annexure-2)

◆ To remove sour taste from curd, tie it in a muslin cloth and wash it for 3-4 times in plain water. Don't throw away the water; it can be used for rice or for the kneading of the dough.

◆ If the curd to be used for making *'raita'* has turned too sour, just hang it in a piece of muslin cloth till all the water drains out. Now mix in enough milk till the required consistency is reached. The sour curd will taste as good as fresh.

◆ Setting the curd during cold season is a pain but some people just can't do without their daily supply of curds. For setting curds during winter, put a little hot water in the casserole and keep the curd bowl in it.

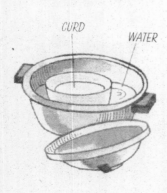

CURD   WATER

◆ Add a teaspoon of corn flour to a small quantity of curd and mix with warm milk. The curd will be thicker and set faster especially during the winter. (See Annexure-6)

◆ If you run out of tomatoes, use the tomato soup powder for the curry. It will taste just as good.

◆ Instead of deep-frying cashew nuts, roast them. They taste better and remain fresh longer. Needless to add that the calories saved by roasting could do a good turn to your body.

◆ It always happens when one is trying to use the mixie or the oven. What happens when you are in the midst of making mayonnaise and the electricity fails? Do you rant and rave? Well, don't, just add a boiled and mashed potato to make the mayonnaise thick.

CLEANING TIPS

Stuck with a dirty 'karahi' or a greasy kitchen sink? Are you unable to find a solution to that dirty stain on your precious wedding gift of expensive bone china set? Or is it the burnt residue on your cooking utensils that bothers you? Well, there is no reason to fret. In this section, there are many tips to help you tide over your problem. Here is wishing you a happy scrubbing and a super clean as well as gleaming kitchen.

◆ To remove stains from utensils, mix bleaching powder in a tub of water and dip the utensils for a while. Wash them with detergent powder later.

◆ To clean a vessel, which is too oily, try cleaning with a few drops of vinegar.

◆ Although we hardly use copper or brass utensils, these days, there are some heirlooms that we like to maintain. Our grandmothers kept their copper and brass vessels gleaming by rubbing them with half a lemon dipped in salt. The vessels can be washed with soap water, after that.

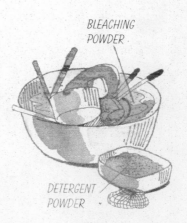

BLEACHING POWDER

DETERGENT POWDER

◆ To add a sheen to the stainless steel utensils, put a few teaspoons of bleach into 500 ml of water and soak the utensils in this solution for a while. This will loosen the deposits on them and brighten them up, too.

BAKING SODA

◆ Rusty knives are an eyesore. To clean rusty knives, stick the blades into an onion and leave for some time.

◆ If the rice is burnt while cooking and you want to clean the inside of the cooker without much effort, place the bottom half of the cooker in a basin of cold water for 5-7 minutes. The residue will dislodge itself.

◆ For sparkling results, rinse delicate bone china and precious glass in water with a dash of vinegar in it.

◆ Yellowed crockery is every homemaker's nightmare. Wash your crockery with baking soda or soda bicarb, for sparkling results.

◆ Stubborn grease can ruin a perfect day. Use aluminum foils of the tablets to clean greasy vessels. They don't leave any scratches, either.

◆ Rubbing plastic containers with oil before placing food in them prevents stains.

◆ To clean the vessel in which milk, *masala* or rice has dried and left a stubborn residue along the edges, rinse out the vessel and keep upside down on a flat surface so that no air escapes. The hard caked dirt comes off in a few seconds.

◆ After extracting sour limejuice, dry the peels in the sun. Grind the dried peels to a powder and use it for washing utensils. Your utensils will sparkle. The benefits don't end here. You can mix the powder with gram flour and use it as a face scrubber as well.

◆ To remove stubborn stains from utensils, soak them in water with a little bleach. Wash them the next day and watch them shine.

◆ To remove burnt food particles from aluminum vessels, rub them with sandpaper. I don't really recommend that you do it often because the sandpaper is likely to leave scratches on the vessels.

◆ Washing ice trays with hot soap water will prevent them from sticking to the floor of the freezer compartment.

◆ Tea and coffee stains can be removed from utensils by rubbing a little salt over them and washing after a few minutes.

PLASTIC VESSEL

COMMON SALT

- To clean stained sinks, use a polythene scrub with Vim and a drop of coconut oil. Scrub in circular motions for a spotless sink.

- For a sparkling kitchen sink and bright tiles, rub a mixture of bleaching powder and water thoroughly, over the tiles. Leave overnight. Rinse with plain water in the morning to get gleaming tiles.

- To remove rust from strainers, warm them on high heat and dust thoroughly. The rust will disappear.

- Add a handful of common salt to the washing powder while cleaning vessels, for better results.

- You must have heard of many uses of the banana peel but here is an unusual one. To clean greasy pots and pans, rub them with the inner side of a banana peel.

- To add sparkle to your china cups, boil them in water to which baking soda has been added.

- Eggs, onions and garlic can leave a horrible smell on the utensils. Utensils smelling of garlic, onion or eggs should be cleaned with salt and washed with cold water to remove the odour.

- Here is a solution to your burnt pan problem. Cover the bottom of your badly burnt pan with a thick layer of soda bicarbonate; add a little water and leave to soak overnight. In the morning, the burnt bits will come off easily.

- Have you ever smelt the can in which you store edible oil? It is most likely to smell quite awful besides being sticky. Rinse oil cans with soap nuts *(reetha)* powder and sour curd along with a little water and wash well. The can will neither retain the smell or the stickiness of oil.

BAKING SODA

CHINA CUPS

- To clean stainless steel vessels stained by hard or salt water, put a small quantity of *'idli'* or *'dosa'* batter into them and add water up to the brim. Keep aside for 24 hours and then wash. The vessels will sparkle again.

- For easy removal of sticker labels from stainless steel vessels, run a burning candle along the edges of the label.

- Used oil is excellent for removing stickers, labels from stainless steel utensils.

- Add a few drops of glycerine to water in which glass bottles are to be boiled. The bottles will clean more easily and won't crack, either.

- Here is another tip for cleaning burnt pans. Soaking them in cold water overnight and then bringing to a boil can clean burnt pans.

- To clean dirty, greasy, kitchen dusters, boil them in soap and washing soda solution. Add some paraffin mixture after removing from the gas and boil again for 20 minutes.

- Brass utensils will clean faster if rubbed with a mixture of mud and lemon juice.

- If there are tough stains on non-stick pans, fill the pan with a cup of water; add half a cup of vinegar and 2 tablespoons of soda bicarb. Boil for 10 minutes, dry and grease lightly with salad oil.

- To clean greasy aluminium *'karahi'*, use sandpaper.

- Spread an old sheet of newspaper while cleaning vegetables to make cleaning up easier.

- If the kitchen sink gets blocked, add some pieces of crystals of salt (not the powdered salt) and leave overnight.

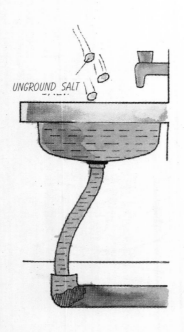

- Plastic plates get awfully soiled due to grease and easily acquire turmeric stains. Cleaning plastic plates with wheat flour will make them sparkle and also remove turmeric stains.

- Cleaning grease is not an easy task. It leaves a sticky residue even after an all-out effort. To clean a greasy grill, sprinkle it with soda bicarb and clean.

- To wash a greasy pan, rub it with some gram flour and wash with soap and water. The grease will come off easily.

- To remove the *'eggy'* smell from crockery, rub it with used tea leaves or rinse with a little vinegar.

- If the inside of an aluminium vessel is stained, boil water along with a little vinegar for about $1/2$ an hour. Then wash thoroughly.

- Rub kitchen tables and work surfaces with lemon juice or lemon rinds to remove grease.
- To shine brass and copper vessels, use lime with a little ash.
- Clean stained melamine crockery by soaking it for half an hour in a tubful of hot water to which 2 cupfuls of liquid bleach has been added. You may not believe this but just try it out; stains as old as 20 years can be removed in this manner.

GADGET TIPS

With the age of automation dawning on the civilization, most kitchens are now crowded with various implements to help the housewife cope with the tremendous task of satiating the hunger of her family. Along with the advent of the gadgets, came the problem of cleaning and maintenance. To help you cope with the task of upkeep, here are several handy tips.

- Fridges need cleaning, too. An easy method for cleaning them is to mix a teaspoon of soda bicarbonate in a cup of water. Apply this on the inner and outer sides of the fridge to make it easy for cleaning.
- To sharpen a blunt knife, rub the tip with salt, cautiously. Cautiously, not because you will spoil the knife but because you may hurt yourself.
- To clean the inside of a microwave oven without scratching the surface, sprinkle baking soda on a damp cloth and gently wipe off the food stains.
- If the flame of your gas stove has turned yellow because of burnt food deposits on the burner, rub it with sandpaper and blow off any powdery waste. The flame will burn bright and blue, once again.
- Clean your gas stove with an old nylon stocking dipped in undiluted washing liquid.
- To open the blocked holes of gas burners, place them in a steel bowl containing a cup of water and

SODA BICARBONATE
FREEZER
WATER

a teaspoon of washing soda. Leave overnight and wash with hot water. Dry immediately.

Don't throw away used toothbrushes. I found a whole range of uses for them. Use a little toothpaste and a used toothbrush to clean the mixer grinder, sunmica-topped tables and other surfaces, to bring a sparkling shine.

To sharpen the blades of your mixie, put a tablespoon of salt and run it for a while. One a month should do the trick.

To get rid of a strong smell of onions or garlic from the mixer jar, pour some salt water into the jar and run the mixer for some time.

To avoid the mixie base from yellowing, rub a lemon half and wipe with a damp cloth.

A mixture of toothpaste and baking soda will remove yellow stains from the refrigerator shelves.

To clean rusty knives, stick the blades into an onion and leave for some time.

To clean burnt fat stains from the inside of an oven, make a paste of soda bicarb and water and apply it to the stained areas. Set the oven on a low temperature for a few minutes. Switch off and clean with a dry cloth. The oven will sparkle beautifully.

ECONOMY TIPS

Along with the responsibility of looking after the gastronomic needs of the family, comes the onus of cutting down the extravagant wastage and pruning the costs. Economizing is an essential factor in housekeeping, these days. Gone are the days of plenty when the women did not mind the wastage. With each passing day, economy in the kitchen becomes more important. For the housewife who walks a tightrope between the budgeted resources and the demands of inflation, it is essential to prune the costs wherever possible. It is also important to derive the maximum mileage from the available resources. Here are some valuable tips to make her an effective finance manager.

◆ When mint leaves are available in plenty, dry them in sun, powder and add rock salt and cumin powder to it. Store in an airtight container and use it to garnish curd, *raita, dahi wadas,* etc.

◆ Fuel is expensive and should be conserved. To do that, we need to find ways and means of cooking faster. To cook *'dal'* faster, add a few drops of mustard oil to it, while cooking.

◆ To make lemons last longer, rub a little coconut oil on them and place them in an open tray in the fridge. They will last as long as a month. This tip is especially useful during the summer season when the price of lemons go up considerably.

◆ If a lemon is warmed before it is squeezed, the juice will flow more readily. When only a small amount of lemon juice is required, pierce a hole with a skewer and extract the required amount. Wrap the lemon in foil and refrigerate it.

◆ To get more juice out of lemons, put them in hot water before squeezing them.

◆ Anyone can grow mint. It can be grown in pots, too. Put sprigs of mint leaves bought from the market, in water for 2 days. Plant them in soil, they will grow very rapidly.

◆ Add $1/2$ a teaspoon of sugarcane juice to old and dried up pickle. It will taste as delicious as fresh pickle.

◆ Coconut milk when kept overnight in the fridge forms a white layer on top. Don't throw this layer as it can be used to fry mutton or chicken, instead of oil. Not only do you get to prevent wastage, the mutton and chicken get a delicious flavour, too.

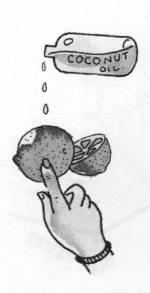

◆ Using less oil for frying is not only economical but beneficial for health, too. Less oil will be consumed while deep-frying, if you add $1/2$ a teaspoon of salt to the oil.

◆ Leftovers are a big problem and the homemaker should be able to recycle them, for optimum benefit. Leftover chutney makes excellent filling for cutlets.

◆ Leftover pickles can be used as fillings for stuffed *'parathas'*.

- Leftover meat or vegetable make excellent filling for *'parathas'*. Just add some chopped onions, coriander leaves and green chillies to bring in a fresh taste. The same mixture can be used for sandwich filling or as a sandwich toast filling.

- To boil potatoes faster, add a little turmeric powder and oil to the water.

- Potatoes can be boiled in a jiffy when a little vinegar is added to the water.

- Don't throw away the butter paper wrapper of the bread or butter. Butter wrappers can be used for lining the baking tray.

- Scrape off the milk cream from the bottom and the sides of a vessel in which the milk has been boiled and knead chapatti dough or prepare a soup in the vessel. Less fat will be required besides making the cleaning of the vessel easier.

- Green peas are cheap in winter and can be preserved in the fridge for 6-10 months, for use in summer. Preserving peas is quite a simple process and anyone can do it. Bring water to boil with a pinch of salt. Add the peas. Let them boil for 1 second. Strain the water and immerse the peas in ice cold water for 2 seconds. Strain again and pack them into airtight polythene packets before placing them in the freezer.

- Another method of storing green peas is to tie the shelled green peas in a cloth and dip in boiling water for 3 minutes. Dry under the fan till the extra moisture is removed and then pack into airtight jars or sealed packets. Freeze and use later. They will keep for up to 2 years. Easy, isn't it?

- Don't throw away the canned fruit base. Save the liquids from the canned fruits and thicken them with corn flour. Heat and serve as sweet sauce for cakes and puddings.

- To use up the leftover syrup of *rasogullas* and gulab jamuns, boil; add *'bundi'* or plain *'sev'* with 3 tablespoons of condensed milk and $1/4$ teaspoon cardamom powder, to make delicious *'laddoos'* out of it.

◆ Use the last bit of tomato sauce in the bottle by adding a little limejuice, shaking well and substituting for tomatoes in the curries.

◆ To use residual chilli sauce, add a little olive oil, some vinegar and seasoning to taste. Mix well and use it as salad dressing.

◆ When the chilli sauce bottle is almost over, add a little limejuice, shake well and use it as a salad dressing.

◆ To get that little bit extra from your gas cylinder, shake it vigorously and place it horizontally for a minute or two. You will be able to get enough fuel for making your cup of tea.

◆ Do not soak *'urad dal'* for more than 1 hour when you are making *'medu wadas'*. They will not absorb much oil this way.

◆ To 5 kg basmati rice of cheaper variety, add 1 kg very good quality basmati rice. Sprinkle a little oil and mix well with your hands. Store in an airtight tin for 6 months. The entire rice will taste like a superior quality one.

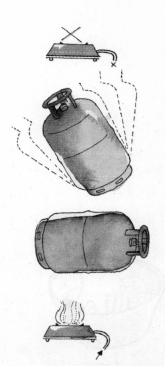

◆ After mincing meat, put a crust of bread through the mincer to push out the residual meat. You will be surprised to see how much meat can be retrieved in this manner.

◆ After making *'paneer'* at home, use the whey for mixing dough. It gives nutritious and soft *'chapatis'*.

◆ Roughly grated core of cabbage can be used for salads and soups. It can also be used for coleslaw.

◆ To leftover cooked rice, add finely chopped onions, chilli powder and salt to taste. Mash well and make small stars out of the mixture and dry in the hot sun. Now, store them in an airtight container. These can be deep fried and eaten as snacks or as a substitute for *'papads'*.

◆ Cornflakes powder makes a wonderful substitute for breadcrumbs. Just put cornflakes on a plastic bag and press them down with a rolling pin.

◆ Aluminium foils are quite expensive. Most of us throw the foil away after a single use. The fact is that is can be reused by washing it after use. Rinse it in hot water and drip dry.

GRAM FLOUR PASTE

SALADS

PAKORAS

RECYCLING TIPS

Leftovers are a common problem that is faced by most homemakers, especially the ones who are new at the game. Most often, the leftovers are thrown away or given away because one doesn't know what to do with it. A little imagination a·d creativity combined with a little skill can often work wonders. Most of the food that is leftover can easily be turned into a delicious dish.

Salads

Leftover pieces of tomatoes can be made into a puree and used to flavour the curry. Other items like onions; cucumbers, green chillies, radish or carrot can be mixed in a paste of gram flour and fried to give delicious *'pakoras'*. They can also be chopped fine and mixed with curd to make a *'kuchumber'*. (See Annexure-3)

Raitas

The leftover *raita* gets soured very quickly as it contains salt and fermentation takes place in the curd. Delicious *'kadhi'* can be prepared from the raita. Remove the potatoes that are in the *raita*. Beat the sour curd; add red chilli powder, coriander powder and some water to it. Besan *'pakoras'* can be added to the *kadhi*. The potato pieces, which have been removed from the raita, can be turned into a delicious potato curry.

Dals

LEFTOVER DAL

PARATHAS OR PURIS

Leftover *'dal'* can be used in many ways. It can be used to knead the dough for making tasty *'parathas'* or *'puris'*. It can be dried up and used as a filling or thinned and made into a soup. Leftover *'rajmah'* can be dried; seasoning added and a fresh salad can be made out of it by adding some onions, green chillies, coriander leaves and tomatoes.

Rice

Plain boiled rice can be made into a tasty *pulao* by frying some onions, adding spices like coriander powder, *jeera* powder, green chillies, tomatoes and coriander leaves.

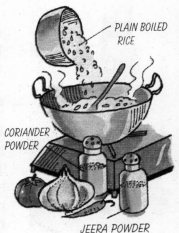

PLAIN BOILED RICE

CORIANDER POWDER

JEERA POWDER

It can also be used to make delicious *idlis*. Mash the rice; add lightly roasted semolina and sour curd in equal proportions. Add water to get a batter like mixture. Add a pinch of cooking soda and salt. Temper with mustard seeds, curry leaves, broken red chillies and *urad dal*. Steam and get soft *idlis*.

Leftover rice can be recycled in another delicious method. Mash the rice; add *jeera* and asafoetida powder, a little salt and some red chilli powder. Now make small 'papads' out of it and dry them in the sun. When the 'papads' are absolutely dry, store them in an airtight container. They can be fried and served as snacks.

Chapatis

With rare exception of those houses where *chapatis* are served straight from the *tawa,* there are always leftovers after every meal and nobody is interested in eating the stale *chapatis*. But these can be put to innovative uses with a little imagination.

JEERA POWDER

CHILLI POWDER

ASAFETIDA POWDER

PLAIN BOILED RICE

PAPAD

Make a thin paste of *besan*. Add chopped onions, coriander leaves, green chillies, *ajwain* and salt to taste. Coat one side of the *chapati* with this paste and fry on hot *tawa*. Repeat with the other side and you have a fantastic *paratha,* which will be much in demand from every member of the house.

Break the *chapati* into small pieces and deep-fry them. Top with diced boiled potatoes, curd, and tamarind chutney or plain mint chutney. This makes a delicious snack.

Fold the *chapatis* into rolls and deep fry. Fill the rolls with beans in tomato sauce and you have got fantastic version of Mexican Tortillas.

SQUEEZED
ROSEGOLLAS

CHOPPED
PISTA,
ALMONDS,
CARDAMON
POWDER

If you garnish the fried, *chapati* pieces with onions and green chillies and sprinkle some *'chaat masala'* on them along with a squeeze of the lemon, you will come up with a tongue tingling *'chaat'*.

Sweets

If you are left with *rosogollas,* that have no takers, try this recipe and you will have a special, fresh sweet dish. Thicken some milk or heat up condensed milk, add sugar, chopped pista, some almonds and cardamom powder. Squeeze the *rosogollas* to remove excess syrup. Drop them in the thickened milk and you will come up with a tasty dish of *rasmalai*.

Dried *khoya* sweets can be crumbled and added to thickened milk and frozen, to make *kulfi*.

Crumble the *khoya* sweets, roast grated fresh coconut lightly, add a little sugar and stir. Add the crumbled *khoya*. Remove from flame and cool. Make laddoos out of the mixture.

STORING TIPS

Are you always pulling out stale and putrid cauliflowers, half rotten tomatoes, shrivelled cucumbers and wrinkled brinjals from the refrigerator? Are you always at sea about storage of the valuable foreign cheese that was gifted by a friend? Do you wonder why the woman next door manages to keep her veggies fresh while yours die on you? Well, here is the secret of her fresh ideas. All you needed to know about storing.

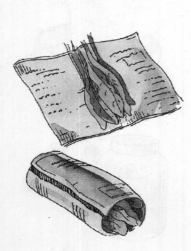

◆ A pinch of corn flour added to the jar of salt will prevent it from getting damp.

◆ Leafy vegetables will remain fresh longer if wrapped in a newspaper and stored.

◆ To preserve coriander leaves or curry leaves, keep them in a muslin cloth bag in the refrigerator. They will remain fresh for a longer time without getting discoloured.

◆ A bay leaf added to the flour container will keep the flour free from moisture.

◆ To store tomatoes longer, place them in the chiller tray. They will freeze partially and last longer.

◆ To keep button mushrooms fresh, drop them into hot, boiling water to which a pinch of salt has been added. Take them out after a minute, drain, cool and store in a plastic, airtight container.

◆ Refrigerate mushrooms and eggplants in paper rather than plastic bags to keep them from developing soft and slimy spots.

◆ To keep herbs fresh, remember that they like carbon di-oxide. So, put them in plastic bags, blow as if it were a balloon and seal tight.

◆ When using only part of a cucumber, tomato or apple, place the remainder unpeeled and cut, side down on a flat, opaque plate. Clear glass exposes the food to light.

◆ To keep Cheddar, Swiss or any other firm cheese from drying, rub soft butter over the cut surfaces and then store in plastic, in the fridge.

◆ Wash and dry salad greens like lettuce. Roll gently in paper towels, dampen the towels slightly, and seal in plastic bags and then store in the refrigerator.

◆ If you store tea leaves for over a month, heat them in an oven at 180 degree Celsius for 10 minutes before filling them into an airtight container. This will keep the leaves fresh.

◆ Sprinkle a little chilli powder and asafoetida on *'papads'* while storing them, to keep ants and insects away.

◆ Green chillies can be preserved up to a month by refrigerating them in thick plastic bags with a small hole punched into it.

◆ Fried *'papads', chips* and biscuits can be kept fresh for a long time by keeping in polythene bags and storing in the fridge.

BAYLEAF

FLOUR

CHILLI POWDER

PAPAD

RICE GRAINS

SALT

♦ Fruits are expensive and one hates to throw away any of them. To increase the shelf life of fruits, refrigerate them in open containers instead of polythene bags.

♦ Soggy and damp salt is a common phenomenon during the monsoon months. A few grains of rice added to salt container will keep the salt dry and smooth flowing.

♦ Green chillies and coriander leaves tend to dry up when stored in the fridge. The coriander leaves sometimes rot and a lot of it has to be thrown away. This can be prevented quite easily if you store coriander leaves and green chillies in paper bags or glass jars in the fridge. They will keep them fresh for a longer time.

♦ Another way to store green chillies longer is to pinch off their stems.

♦ To prevent refined flour from getting spoiled, store it in the refrigerator.

♦ *Paneer* is every vegetarian's delight but it is difficult to keep it in a fresh condition for a long time. To keep *'paneer'* soft for a longer period, keep it in vinegar, tie a piece of muslin to the mouth of the container.

♦ *Paneer* will remain fresh for long if kept in a container filled with water, in the fridge.

♦ *Paneer,* when wrapped in blotting paper, remains fresh and soft for days together on storing in the fridge.

♦ To increase the shelf life of *'paneer'*, store in polythene bags smeared with vinegar.

♦ Here is an interesting way to use up the empty matchboxes. To preserve rice and wheat, place empty matchboxes in the container.

♦ One can save on time by making a quantity of ginger-garlic paste to be used whenever required. To preserve ginger-garlic paste, fry ginger and garlic in oil before grinding and store in the same oil.

♦ Some green vegetables dry up fast and ladyfinger is one such vegetable. To keep ladyfingers fresh for a long time, apply a little mustard oil on them.

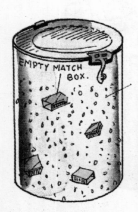

EMPTY MATCH BOX.

RICE OR WHEAT

ASAFETIDA

CHILLI POWDER.

◆ When the fridge is fully stacked, it is difficult to rummage through the lot to hunt out the required item. To find the required stuff easily, store different foods in different coloured plastic bags e.g. Fish in red, meat in yellow, vegetables in green and so on, for easy identification.

◆ To store chilli powder for a longer duration, keep a piece of asafoetida in the container.

◆ The shelf life of spices like cinnamon, cloves and black pepper can be increased when stored together in an airtight container.

◆ To prevent the bread from getting spoilt, store it in the fridge along with a few pieces of potatoes.

◆ To preserve the aroma of coffee powder, keep it in an airtight container and store it in the fridge.

◆ Dry fruits are expensive and no one likes to have them spoilt. To preserve dry fruits, add a couple of cloves to the container.

◆ Store tomatoes in deep freezer to keep them fresh for months.

◆ To keep ginger fresh, dig a hole in the garden and bury the ginger pieces. They can also be put in a flowerpot.

◆ While storing camphor, add a few peppercorns. Camphor can be stored for a long period in this manner.

◆ Wrap sweet limes and oranges in brown paper bags and store in the fridge to keep them fresh for 15-20 days.

LIME WATER
MUSTARD
OIL

◆ Coffee powder and coffee beans will retain their flavour for long if you store them in an airtight container in the fridge.

◆ Eggs can be preserved for a longer duration if they are washed and put slowly in a container full of limewater or mustard oil.

◆ Put 2 or 3 peppercorns in your honey jar. It is a good preservative and also keeps the ants away.

◆ Most of the working women do not have time to go vegetable shopping every day. They generally buy

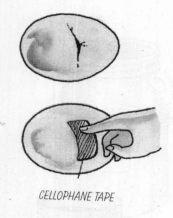

CELLOPHANE TAPE

the week's requirements and store in the fridge. Often it is observed that many vegetables become stale and dry and have to be thrown. Vegetables will remain fresh for a long time if soaked for about 10 minutes in cold water to which a teaspoon of vinegar has been added. After the vegetables are slightly dry, they can be stacked in the fridge.

◆ Use cellophane tape to seal the cracks in eggs. They will stay as fresh and for as long as the uncracked ones.

◆ If you wish to retain the freshness of asafoetida, pound it with an equal amount of common salt and store.

◆ Tired of soggy biscuits? Here is an easy method to take care of your problem. Place a sugar cube in the biscuit box to keep the biscuits crisp.

ANTI-PEST TIPS

You have guessed it right. Pests can be a big pain. Nowhere do they flourish more than the kitchen stores. If you love stocking up the groceries, watch out for that omnipresent weevil. If you have forgotten to check the containers during the monsoon, don't be surprised if your 'dals' have been reduced to dust and the rice has managed to harbour a host of unwelcome pests. Not to be ignored is the lethal tribe of cockroaches who can survive with a great tenacity, come rain or shine. Dealing with the pests in the kitchen takes a tremendous amount of patience and knowledge. To help you in the onerous task are these hints, which promise you a pest free kitchen.

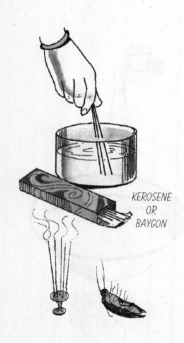

KEROSENE OR BAYGON

◆ Adding some bay leaves to stored raw rice will keep worms at bay while lending it a delicate fragrance.

◆ Dip 'agarbattis' in Baygon or kerosene and then light them. The fumes will repel mosquitoes and flies.

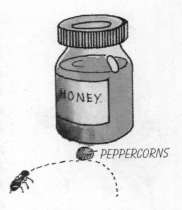

PEPPERCORNS

◆ To get rid of pests in dals, add a small piece of asafoetida.

◆ Add 3-4 cloves to the sugar container, to keep the ants away.

◆ To de-worm *'rawa'*, spread it on thin *'mulmul'* cloth and sieve after half an hour. The worms will stick to the cloth.

◆ Add a few peppercorns to a bottle of honey to keep ants at bay.

◆ To prevent *'dals'* from being infested with worms, add a little piece of asafoetida to the containers.

◆ Put 6-7 cloves in 1 kg rawa to keep it free from worms.

◆ Mix a little boric powder in rice to prevent infestation by worms.

◆ To protect rice from insects, dry 50 gms of mint leaves, powder them and add to 10 kgs of rice. Not only will it keep the insects at bay, it will also add a delicious flavour to the rice.

◆ Place small pieces of asafoetida in the turmeric and coriander powder containers to protect them from worms.

◆ To keep flies away from the kitchen and dining room, cut an onion into half and keep it in one corner of the room. All the flies will flock to the onion and stay away from the food.

◆ To eliminate the cockroaches from the kitchen, soak a rag in beer and keep it overnight in the kitchen. It will attract the cockroaches and then you can kill them. Happy hunting!

WOODEN
SPOON

PRACTICAL TIPS

Many are the times when a woman wishes that some common sense tips were available to her. Tips that would help her deal with the day-to-day problems that arise while she attends to the multi-faceted chores in the kitchen. The tips that help her deal with these problems are born out of experience. With the joint family system crumbling and giving way to the nuclear family, there are no elderly women of the family, available to help out the younger women. The wisdom born out of years of experience required to deal with these little problems is often missing. The tips given here are taken from the books of several experienced women of the older generations who have learnt through trial and error process of learning.

◆ Did you get the shock of your life when you used your new electric stove? Using wooden spatula or spoon while cooking on an electric stove will go a long way in preventing the nasty shocks.

◆ Summers can be a troublesome time. The heat and the power cuts add to cause dual trouble. Right from the sweat and grime in the kitchen, to the milk getting curdled at every given opportunity. You can prevent the milk from getting spoiled by adding 4-5 grains of paddy to a glassful of milk.

GLYCERINE

MILK

◆ Each time you leave the milk on the stove, does it betray you by boiling over? It always happens. The moment you turn your back on the milk sitting on the gas stove, it boils over. To prevent milk from boiling over, apply a little glycerine to the rim of the utensil.

◆ Burnt smell in the milk can ruin even the most perfect cup of tea or coffee. Before boiling milk, rinse the container with water. This prevents it from getting burnt.

◆ If the milk has got burnt, despite all your efforts, pour it into another vessel, add a pinch of soda bicarb and bring it to a boil. The burnt smell will vanish.

◆ It is amazing how the water will boil over and overflow when you are preparing the rice or noodles. It not only creates a mess but can put off the flame of the gas stove, making it dangerous, too. To prevent the water from boiling over while cooking rice, macaroni or noodles, coat the rim of the vessel with vanaspati.

◆ There are numerous tips for easy peeling of the garlic, here's another one. To peel garlic flakes easily, wash and soak them in cold water for around an hour. You can use the same water while grinding the garlic.

GARLIC

◆ To avoid garlic skin from sticking to your hands while peeling it, soak the garlic flakes in a cupful of water for 5 minutes before flaking.

◆ Ah! Those smelly hands. All your friends as well as foes get to know when you cook fish in your kitchen. Rub a little mustard powder on your hands after handling onions or fish, to get rid of the smell.

◆ Another smell that women hate on their hands is the strong odour of onions and garlic. To remove the offensive odour from your hands, rub them with salt or a lemon peel.

◆ Tears and onions have a great affinity for each other. It is decades since I began cooking, but I still have the tears rolling down my cheeks, whenever I chop the onions. Mainly because I forget to heat the knife before chopping onions. Don't forget to do so, if you don't want to shed the tears.

◆ Peeling garlic is a messy business. Here are a few tips on flaking garlics without the mess. Garlic flakes can be peeled very easily if placed in the sun for a while before peeling.

◆ One major problem that novices find themselves facing, when they cut onions is that the slices separate. Leave the root ends of onions intact while slicing them. The slices will be held together till you finish cutting.

SUGAR

- Instead of laboriously peeling garlic flakes, wash and grate them. The skins will be left behind on top of the grater while the garlic paste will emerge through the grater at the bottom, soft and ready to use.

- Have you ever observed how the custard becomes lumpy when you try to dissolve it? To prevent lumps from forming while dissolving custard powder, dissolve a little sugar in water and add it to the custard powder.

- My teenaged daughter loves to make desserts. She is a wizard at unmoulding the desserts made out of gelatine. Here is a trick to help you, too. To unmould gelatine desserts, wrap a hot towel around the hot mould for 15 seconds, then unmould it with a quick, downward snap on a plate.

- Green looks good on the dining table but most vegetables lose their colour when they are cooked. Green vegetables will retain their colour if you sprinkle some sugar on them while cooking.

- Kneading the dough requires professional handling. I have seen real messy hands and kitchens after the 'operation kneading' is over. Next time, try kneading the *'atta'* in a non-stick pan, so that the flour doesn't stick to the vessel.

- The sight of the excess oil dripping from the potato chips or bitter gourds is enough to deter the bravest of hearts. To get rid of excess oil in fried vegetables, sprinkle a little gram flour over it.

- After you're deep-frying, you will generally find that the oil becomes cloudy. To clear up oil, which has become cloudy, fry a few potato slices in it. The remaining particles will settle down at the bottom.

POTATO
SLICES

CLOUDY OIL

- To prevent oil from turning an unsightly brown while frying, drop a marble sized ball of tamarind or a betel leaf into it.

- A layer of fat swimming on the soup—sounds unappetizing, isn't it? It is quite common to find this sight in the soup bowls. Prevent this by skimming the fat from the top of soup. Use a sheet of paper towel. It will absorb the excess fat, immediately.

- The chicken, mutton and dals cooked in earthenware have a delicious flavour. But handling the earthen pots is quite a difficult proposition because they break so easily. To prevent breakage of earthenware when heated, rub the exteriors of the earthen pan with an onion before use.

- There is another way to skim fats from soups. Drop in some ice cubes. The fat will cling to the ice cubes and can be easily removed.

- I have a friend who likes the taste of curries, which are cooked, with a generous helping of fried onions but she abhors the smell of the frying onions. If you are like her and don't like the smell of onions, add a little sugar while frying them.

- Botulism, which occurs in stale tinned food, is a dangerous thing. To test the freshness of tinned food, put a drop or two of water on the lid of the tin and puncture at that very spot. If the water is sucked in, the food in the tin is fresh.

- Over-ripe tomatoes can be put to use by dipping in salty cold water. Leave them overnight and they will be firm and fresh, the next day.

- *'Dosa'* batter tends to get sour and stale when kept in the fridge for a long time. Keep the batter without adding salt and it will remain fresh. Take out the required amount add salt and keep out for fermentation.

- When you have unexpected guests turning up at mealtime, increase the quantity of curd and *'raita'* by mixing freshly grated coconut after grinding it to a fine paste.

- Pickles tend to spoil very easily. A lot of precautions and care has to be taken to preserve them. Do not add raw oil to any pickle. Heat the oil until smoky and then cool it before use. This will prevent the formation of fungus in the pickle.

- Keep the *'idli'* and *'dhokla'* batter in a tightly closed pressure cooker. The batter will ferment faster. This method can also be used to sprout *'matki'* and *'moong'*.

- I almost considered turning into a vegetarian because I found it so tough to cut raw meat. What I didn't know is that raw meat can be sliced easily with a knife dipped in hot water.

- The cutting and cleaning of small and medium size fish, prawn or vegetable will be much easier if an old pair of scissors is used instead of a knife. The blades of the scissors can be sharpened like a kitchen knife.

- Fish has a bad habit of spluttering when you fry it. This causes untold misery to the young housewife. Before frying fish, add a pinch of turmeric to the oil. This prevents the oil from spluttering out of the pan onto your hands.

- I am one of those who enjoy eating seafood only in restaurants because it is so difficult to clean the prawns, shellfish and crabs, at home. But cooks tell me that there is a very simple solution to this problem. Deep freeze the fish and hold it under running water. The shells will open out in a jiffy.

- Breadcrumbs just do not like meat and fish. What else could be the reason that they do not stick to them? They need chilling out. Breadcrumbs will stick better to meat or fish, if you chill them for 20 minutes, before frying.

MUSTARD PASTE

- Bengali housewives knew this trick for ages and hence every Bengali lady applies a little mustard paste to fish pieces to prevent them from breaking.

- If crumbling yolks are your problems, here's a tip. Immerse the knife in cold water before slicing a hard-boiled egg. The yolk will not crumble. You could also try to cut it with a piece of thread.

- To prevent the eggs from cracking while boiling, pierce them with a sharp pin before boiling.

- If you want real fluffy egg whites, refrigerate egg whites before beating them for cakes, ice creams or puddings.

- Fish and odour go together but some just don't like the smell. For odour free fish, soak them in milk and drain or wash them with vinegar.

- To cook a perfect '3 minute egg', place the egg in a saucepan of cold water and bring to a boil. As soon as the water reaches boiling point, turn off the heat. As soon as the water stops boiling the egg is done to perfection.

- After hard-boiled eggs have been cooked, run cold water over them, and leave them for a while in the cold water. This will prevent the formation of that unattractive gray ring around the yolk.

- Ever noticed how awful the cooker looks after you have been boiling eggs or potatoes in it. If you add a piece of tamarind or lemon peel in the cooker while boiling the eggs or steaming the 'idlis' the cooker will not turn black.

- Lemon juice has the property of taking off the odour from almost anything. Whether it is the fish or the egg, a little lemon juice does the trick. For those of you who do not like the eggy smell in an omelette, here is a hint. Add 4-5 drops of lemon juice to the egg while beating it for an omelette to get rid of the eggy smell.

- Pure saffron is costlier than gold and one cannot afford to waste it. To extract the real flavour of saffron, first roast and crush it and then mix it with a little limejuice or sour curd for spicy dishes and with cold milk for desserts or sweets.

- If you like your *'dosa'* crisp, add a teaspoon of *'tur dal'* and some 'methi' seeds while soaking rice for *'dosa'*.

- There are many ways of making a *dosa* crisp, here is another method. Add a handful of *'poha'* to dosa batter for crisp *dosas*.

◆ Cakes look good when there is a nice gloss on them. To add a nice glaze to the cake in a very inexpensive manner, sprinkle a little castor sugar over the cake while it is being baked.

◆ To get rid of the eggy smell in cakes, add 1-tablespoon honey to the cake batter while beating it. The cake will taste better, too.

◆ If you like your peas to look green and fresh, remember this tip. Green peas will retain their original colour if you add a pinch of sugar while boiling them.

◆ It is embarrassing to serve a fruit salad with bananas that have turned black. You could, however, prevent them from turning black by putting the pieces in a bowl of water. The same trick works for potatoes, too.

◆ Sticky ladyfinger dishes are a cook's nightmare. To prevent the *bhindis* from becoming sticky, toss the chopped pieces in a tablespoon of lemon juice, before cooking.

◆ Everyone loves eating cauliflowers but only a housewife knows that creepy and crawly pests also love eating it. One easy way to remove those pests hiding in the flower is to soak the cauliflower in salt water for about ten minutes. The pests will float on top.

◆ Add a teaspoon of turmeric powder to a bowl of water in which chopped vegetables are immersed. Small insects and worms will float at the top.

◆ Fed up of the sticky sticker on the utensil, just heat it gently and the sticker will come off easily.

◆ Blocked tea strainers can become a nuisance. When a stainless steel tea strainer gets blocked, heat it on a gas flame and wash off with soap water.

◆ This tip came from a friendly neighbour when my husband was posted in the South. Leftover *'idli'* batter will not turn sour if you add a piece of banana leaf or a few ladyfinger stems to it.

◆ To get a natural colouring and nutritional benefit, add a cupful of grated beetroot or carrot to the coconut while making *'barfi'*.

◆ If you have peeled more potatoes than required, keep them in cold water to which one teaspoon vinegar has been added. They will keep fresh for 4-5 days. I won't recommend peeling the potatoes and keeping them in water, though because there won't be any food value left in them after they have been left in the water for some time.

◆ Add a little salt to water in which potatoes are to be boiled, for making cutlets. The potatoes absorb salt better this way.

◆ *Sambars* taste heavenly when those tiny onions are added to them but peeling the tiny onions is a big troublesome job. Necessity is the mother of invention and I am sure someone must have discovered this helpful hint, too. Here it goes. To peel the *'sambar'* onions faster, rub them with a little oil and turmeric powder and keep them in the sun for a few minutes.

◆ This tip came from Vasanthi, my South Indian maid. To make *'sambar'* stay fresh longer; add a few cloves to the *'dal'* while cooking it.

◆ Add 2-3 pieces of potato to the chutney to absorb excess salt.

◆ Artificial food colours should be avoided but when a little colour is required and one wants to avoid the artificial colour, what does one do? Peel a beetroot and cut into tiny pieces. Dry well in the sun and powder it. This can be used as food colour and it is not harmful, either.

◆ I still used my grinding stone because grinding a small quantity of cardamom, in a mixer, is difficult. Then my cousin came over for a visit, she told me to grind it along with a small quantity of sugar. Not only is it easier, it also gives a uniform cardamom flavour.

◆ To find out if the brinjal and bittergourd have too many seeds in them, look at the end opposite the stem. If the perforation there is small, the vegetable will have less seeds. If the perforation is large, it will have more seeds.

◆ Fed up with the jagged cuts on the cake? Use a sewing thread to cut a cake horizontally by holding the thread around the cake and pulling both the ends towards you. Boiled eggs can also be cut using the same method.

◆ Hold peeled banana under cold tap water to prevent discolouration. Alternatively, add some limejuice to them.

◆ My icing was always flawed. It just wasn't firm and would crack up. As a result I almost stopped icing the cakes till I discovered that adding a teaspoon of condensed milk while making the icing really helped.

◆ To keep *'dosas'* fresh, sprinkle a little water on them as soon as you remove them from the pan.

◆ This one is really the ultimate! When I was given this tip, I just couldn't stop laughing. To prevent the dough from sticking to the rolling pin, keep it in the freezer for a few minutes before using it. Not the rolling pin, silly!

◆ If you have run out of green vegetables for salads, just mix some finely chopped onions with fresh, shelled green chanas or boiled *kabuli chana,* and serve. Sprouts are also delicious when seasoned with lemon juice and sugar.

◆ Staying in the South for several years has helped me immensely. The tips for making the best coffee in the world came from the folks next door. For making tasty coffee, drop $1/4$ teaspoon sugar into the filter before adding the coffee and then pour boiling water over it.

◆ Not to be outdone, my Punjabi neighbour provided me with a handy hint for a pleasantly fragrant and refreshing cup of tea. Add an orange peel to the teapot for deliciously flavoured tea.

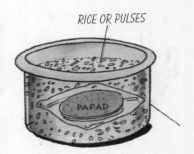

RICE OR PULSES

PAPAD

◆ I have often seen people throwing the residual remains after extracting ghee from butter or cream. In Bengal, we use it up to eat rice with. You can also add sugar to the residue and use it to make sweet or stuffed *'parathas'*.

◆ I have thrown away many packets of *'papads'* before I came across this tip. To prevent *'papads'* from drying and breaking, wrap them in a polythene sheet and store along with rice or pulses.

◆ If you are going for a party and your hands smell of onions, just sprinkle a little mustard powder on them and rub together. After this, just massage in a little rose water and your hands will be left smelling of roses.

◆ Someone must have told you not to use soda because it is not too good for the health. Then what does one do if one has to cook pulses like *Rajmah* or Chana? Dried and ground watermelon peels can be used instead of soda bicarb to make the pulses cook faster.

◆ To preserve the white colour of cauliflower, add a teaspoon of milk or milk powder while cooking it.

◆ Summer months can be quite telling on one's nerves and one wants to cool down with a glass of lemon juice. But not everyone has the time to indulge in the task of squeezing out lemons. What you can do is pour lemon juice with sugar and a little salt into ice trays to make cubes, which can be used, for instant lemon juice.

◆ Mushrooms are tasty but one must check whether they are edible, before cooking the lot. To check mushrooms for poison, boil them in water to which garlic flakes are added. If water turns black, it means they are poisonous.

◆ Sprinkle boiling water on mushrooms while sautéing, to prevent them from shrinking.

POISONOUS MUSHROOMS

SILVER COINS.

NAIL POLISH REMOVER →

◆ Oh! Those awful stickers on the new vessels! They just don't seem to go away. Stickers from new vessels can be removed with nail polish remover.

◆ After reading about a few cases of mushroom poisoning, I almost gave up eating them although I love them. And then I found this tip - to test mushrooms for edibility, boil them in water with 2-3 cloves of garlic. If the water turns brown or black, they are not edible.

◆ It is surprising how many tips you come across when you are looking for a particular one. I came across several hints about detecting the edibility of a mushroom. Here is another one. Put a silver coin in the dish you are cooking mushroom in. If it turns black, the mushrooms are poisonous.

◆ Quite often we find one glass stuck within another one and it is quite a pain separating them. When one vessel is stuck to another, place them in boiling water and they will separate.

◆ So many recipes require only half an onion and what does one do with the other half? If only half an onion is needed, cut it in half before you peel it. The unpeeled half will keep much longer until it is needed.

◆ The gases, which form inside the tinned stuff, sometimes do not allow the lid to open easily. If you have difficulty in opening a jam or pickle bottle, just pierce a hole in the lid. The gases will escape and the lid will open without any problem.

SILVER COINS

◆ How do you set curd without the 'starter'? If you have run out of curd, to set fresh curd, put a silver coin in warm milk. You will get thick curd.

◆ If the jelly does not turn out well, don't despair. Just add curd, roughly half the quantity of the jelly and sugar to taste. Churn it in the mixie. Set it and serve as a novel dessert.

◆ Chopping dry fruits is tedious. It is easier to cut dry fruits if you dip the scissors first in tepid water.

◆ Spreading two sheets of grease proof paper over and under the cake tin before baking the cake will prevent the cake from burning.

◆ Kitchen scissors come in very handy while dealing with several matters like trimming the edges of bread slices.

◆ To get the tomato sauce out easily from a new bottle, use a straw.

◆ Ever noticed how some of the vegetables in a curry get cooked in a jiffy while the others take ages to cook? To ensure even cooking, cut all the vegetables in a uniform size.

◆ Limp and damp tomatoes in a salad can look and taste quite awful. To get firm tomatoes for salads, keep them in a bowl of iced water for some time.

◆ Here is another tip for a nice platter of salad. To keep the salad fresh, chill the serving bowl before serving the salad in it.

◆ It isn't always necessary to make fancy dressings for the salad, especially when you don't have the time to do so. To make a quick salad dressing, blend a cup of curd with a little limejuice and seasoning and toss the salad into it.

◆ To make the holes of a sieve smaller, paint the sieve net from both sides and allow it to dry.

◆ Champagne and wine bottles should be tilted for a while in order to prevent the cork from breaking into pieces.

◆ I hated the fact that I could never break a coconut properly. The coconut often broke into two halves with uneven edges. And then I saw a person drawing a line with wet fingers around its midriff. He explained that the coconut would break at the

RICE   LEMON

marked line. And so it did. Since then, I have been firm about drawing the line.

♦ Add the juice of half a lemon while preparing rice to get whiter grains.

♦ If you want to eat a piping hot meal, place a soup plate of steaming hot water under your plate. The meal will be hot and appetising within no time. The hot water can later be used as a finger bowl to get the grease off your fingers.

♦ To freshen stale bread, sprinkle a little milk over it and place it in a moderately hot oven, for 15 minutes. The crust will be crisper and the bread tastier.

♦ While keeping *'chapatis'* in a container, place a few pieces of ginger in it. It keeps the *'chapatis'* softer and fresher.

♦ To prevent the *'moong dal halwa'* form sticking to the pan, fry one-tablespoon flour in the pan before you prepare the halwa.

♦ Pressure cook tomatoes with salt and cool. Churn in a mixie and strain the juice. Deep freeze the tomato juice in an ice tray. Store the cubes in a plastic bag in the freezer. Use them to make tomato soup, vegetable gravies etc. The cubes can also be used when you run out of tomatoes. They are an economical substitute when the tomato prices become prohibitive.

HOT WATER

♦ To spread butter on a toast during winters is really a hard task. Dip the butter knife in hot water and scoop out the butter.

♦ Serve steaming hot dinner rolls by placing a hot ceramic tile at the bottom of the bread basket. Place the rolls over it and cover with a napkin.

MASALA FACTS

If ever you thought that the typical Indian spices were used just to spice up your life, you can't be farther than the truth. Although they do help in bringing in some flavour into dull lives, essentially, they were used because of their curative properties. A little knowledge about the values of the condiments one uses definitely helps in applying the right condiment for the right effect. Next time you use the condiments, you will actually be aware of its use in maintaining your health.

Spices are not used just for flavour or taste; they also contain many useful elements and are often of medicinal value. For instance, cumin seeds and *ajwain* contain iron and protein, while mustard contains phosphorus, *methi* (fenugreek) contains calcium, and coriander seeds contain vitamin A.

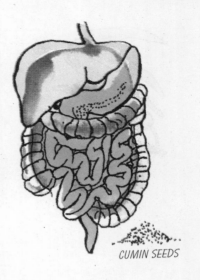

CUMIN SEEDS

Cumin Seeds (Jeera)

It aids digestive process and controls gas formation in the stomach. It also acts as a remedy for stomachache. It is also an invaluable cure for vomiting, diarrhoea and lack of appetite. Its oil contains cummic aldehyde, which helps in the digestion of proteins contained in cereals and pulses. This oil can be artificially converted into thymol, which is antiseptic and acts as a controller of worms. When jeera is added to vegetables, the cellulose content in them becomes softer and the hemi-cellulose becomes soluble, thus making them easy to digest.

Coriander Seeds (Dhania)

Prevents burning sensation in the stomach and facilitates the excretion of unwanted matter through urine. It promotes appetite, cleans up the stomach and helps in the digestion of fried food material. A paste made up of the seeds ground with some water and applied to the forehead can relieve headache. Soak in water overnight, strain and mix with curdled milk and use it to check diarrhoea. Regular use of this spice prevents joint pains and improves eyesight.

WATER   CORIANDER SEED

Aniseed (Saunf)

It is normally used for curries made of tomatoes, green mangoes and gram flour. It alleviates acidity, lack of appetite and amoebiasis. It also helps in curing chronic headaches and improves eyesight. Aniseed helps in combating dry skin, burning sensation while passing urine and blisters in the mouth. It also strengthens the organs like kidney, eyes and lungs to fight the diseases.

Turmeric (Haldi)

Turmeric is the kitchen's wonder medicine. It is a blood purifier, air purifier and complexion-improving element. Recent research has also found that it can be used to fight cancer. It has very good antibiotic properties and when used in cooking vegetables, it prevents food poisoning. It is very useful in cold, cough, breathing problems, backaches and intestinal swellings.

Red Chillies (Lal Mirchi)

It promotes the production of saliva and digestive enzymes thus reducing indigestion. The capsine existing in red chillies, aid in sharpening the sense of taste and aroma. It also helps in fighting cancer.

Ginger (Adrak)

It is very helpful in promoting the taste, flavour of any dish. It also aids in digestion. It can be used in its dry form also. Inclusion of ginger in the spices makes the tough food cook faster. It eliminates cough, gas and heavy sensation in the stomach. Eating a little ginger with salt just before a meal improves the appetite. Doctors recommend its use by heart patients. It is a good cure for breathing problems, coughs, throat inflammation and fever.

Mustard Seeds (Sarson)

It alleviates constipation and combats the intestinal worms. Its anti-cough properties help in controlling chronic coughs.

Caraway Seeds (Ajwain)

It has digestive, germicidal properties. It combats bad odour and stomachaches. It is also useful in curing chronic coughs, liver enlargements, breathing problems and skin problems. It can be used to control vomiting, hook worms and thread worms. Its efficacy in controlling heart ailments is under research.

FENUGREEK

Asafoetida (Hing)

It is the resin derived from a tree. Its affectivity in controlling the unease and flatulence after heavy meals is renowned. It also controls stomach cramps and promotes the health of the liver. Traditionally, it was used to cure the worms in the stomach, epilepsy, asthma, intestinal swelling etc.

Fenugreek Seeds (Methi)

Used mainly in vegetable curries and pickles, it is rich in calcium, proteins, iron, chlorine, and phosphorus. Therefore it is very nutritious and strength producing spice. It also increases the secretion of digestive enzymes. Fenugreek seeds are very effective in curing weakness, joint pains, headaches, diabetes and loss of appetite. Regular use also helps in controlling body weight and blood cholesterol level.

Onion Seeds (Kalonji)

Contains tannin, aluminium etc. Helps in digestion, fights germs, combats gas formation. Lactating mothers can use it to increase the flow of the milk and reduce the heaviness in the lower limbs.

Garlic (Lahsun)

It has been used since age immemorial to cure flatulence. It is also prescribed to lower blood pressure. It forms the base of many medicines for lung disorders and respiratory diseases. Regular intake of garlic can also cure skin blemishes and ailments. A paste made of it can give relief from pain caused by the sting of a scorpion.

Some Useful Tips on How to Make at Home

Garam Masala—*North Indian Style*

Ingredients:
1. Peppercorns   – 20 gms.
2. Cloves   – 10 gms.
3. Cinnamon   – 20 gms.
4. Brown Cardamoms   – 15 gms.
5. Caraway/cumin seeds – 10 gms.

Lightly roast the ingredients on a griddle and pound to a fine powder.

Garam Masala—*Eastern Indian Style*

Ingredients: 1. Green cardamoms 2. Cinnamom 3. Cloves in equal amounts

Lightly roast the ingredients on a griddle and pound to a fine powder.

Sambhar Powder

Ingredients
1. Whole dry red chillies – 25 gms
2. Coriander seeds   – 25 gms
3. Bengal gram   – 10 gms
4. Fenugreek seeds   – 1 tsp
5. Peppercorns   – 1 tsp.

Lightly roast the ingredients on a griddle and pound to a fine powder.

Paneer or Cottage Cheese

Bring to boil 1 litre of milk. Stir continuously. Add the juice of 1 lemon after the milk boils. Stir gently so that the whole milk curdles. Leave it undisturbed for some time and then strain through a muslin cloth. The residue in the cloth should be hung for around $1/2$ an hour. Put it in a dish and put a weight above it so that it acquires a rectangular shape and is around 1 cm. thick.

Khoya

Boil 1 litre milk over high heat until it becomes thick and all the water evaporates. The residue that is left behind is called khoya or mawa.

Tamarind Pulp

Ingredients
1. Tamarind   100 gms
2. Hot water   1 cup

Soak the tamarind in hot water for around 15 minutes. Mix well to dissolve the pulp well and strain.

Chaat Masala

Ingredients
1. Cumin seeds   – 3 tsps (roasted and powdered)
2. Black salt   – 2 tsps
3. Chilli powder   – 1 tsp
4. Amchur powder   – 5 tsps
5. White salt   – $\frac{1}{2}$ tsp
6. Black pepper powder – 1 tsp.

Mix well and serve when required.

Coconut Milk

Mix equal quantity of grated coconut and hot water. After around half an hour, squeeze out the milk.

Idli Batter

Ingredients
1. Rice   – 2 cups
2. Urad dal   – 1 cup

Soak the ingredients overnight. Grind to a coarse paste. Add salt. Mix well and keep aside to ferment.

Dosa Batter

Ingredients
1. Rice   – $2\frac{1}{2}$ cups
2. Urad dal   – 1 cup

Soak the ingredients overnight. Grind to a smooth paste. Add salt. Mix well and keep aside to ferment.

URAD DAL

RICE

SALT

PASTE

Safety Tips While Working in the Kitchen

1. Always wear cotton clothes and avoid synthetic ones.

2. Never wear loose and flowing garments.

3. Always use a pair of tongs to lift a hot vessel from the stove.

4. Do not keep any inflammable substances near the gas cylinder, like a can of kerosene or petrol, etc.

8. In case you suspect a gas leak, never switch on any electrical appliance, but open the windows.

6. Never keep your refrigerator in your kitchen.

7. Never keep burning agarbattis in your kitchen or anywhere in the house, especially when you leave your house.

8. Change your rubber tubing according to its wear and tear.

INFLAMMABLES

Beauty

Beauty

Apart from being proficient in many other things, today's woman has to be conscious about her physical fitness and her looks. In fact, beauty has become a big business, the world over. There is also a growing awareness about the efficacy of the herbal products that have been used by our grandmothers and their grandmothers. As compared to the chemical components in cosmetics, the herbal components do not harm the user and actually have a better effect. No wonder, the world is waking up to the traditional systems of beauty treatments.

SKIN

When the saying - 'Beauty is skin deep' was coined, realization about the importance of skin in the beauty factor must have been the prime focus. Skin takes a very important place in any beauty ritual. The loving care taken during the early years can often delay the process of ageing and the care taken during the later years can work wonders in maintaining a youthful appearance. Skin care, done the right way, can easily enhance the looks of a person. Given here are some traditional beauty rituals, which will definitely go a long way in preserving the beauty of the skin.

◆ Face packs are extremely beneficial for the complexion and smoothness of the skin. Bitter almonds make an excellent face pack when mixed with sandalwood powder and *'multani mitti'*.

◆ Facemasks made with '*dal*' are great softeners for the skin. Grind any *dal* with a pinch of turmeric. Add a few drops of lemon juice and a tablespoon of milk. Apply this paste on the face. Leave it on till dry and then wash off with lukewarm water.

TURMERIC POWDER

MILK

DAL.

◆ It is said that a woman's hand is supposed to be soft, shapely and well maintained because she uses it to express herself. Hard work can rob the hands of their softness. Here is a tip to help you maintain the hands to their optimum condition. For soft palms, apply a mixture of sugar and olive oil and rub for a while before washing it off.

◆ We know that sun robs the skin of its youthful texture and quality yet we can't really prevent facing the sun. Going out in the sun also tans the skin, especially if you have a job that requires frequent trips during the day. If your skin has got badly tanned, apply raw potato juice to get rid of the tan.

◆ To get rid of freckles, grate a radish and extract 2 tablespoon of juice. Mix with equal quantity of buttermilk and apply on the face. Wash off with warm water, after an hour. Use it daily.

◆ Tender coconut water applied on the skin regularly for six months, removes smallpox scars.

◆ Pimples can be a teenager's nightmare. They are easy to sprout and difficult to eradicate. Mix an equal quantity of eau-de-cologne with boiled and cooled lemon juice. Apply this solution over pimples. They will disappear leaving your skin soft and smooth.

◆ If there is one thing that can mar the beauty of eyes, it is the dark circles that form under the eyes. For effective treatment of dark circles under the eyes, place pumpkin slices.

PUMPKIN SLICE

◆ Don't shy away from the humble papaya. It is a wonderful fruit, which has many useful properties. Papaya pulp when applied regularly on the face, cures pimples and blackheads.

◆ For a cleaner complexion, apply sour whey to your face and keep it on for at least 15 minutes. Wash off with lukewarm water. Follow this routine for 15 days.

◆ Rough and dark elbows can be an ungainly sight. If your elbows have become dark and rough, apply groundnut oil mixed with lemon.

◆ Plucking of eyebrows can cause discomfort and pain. Before plucking your eyebrows, lay a hot flannel over the area for several minutes to open the pores. This makes the plucking less painful.

◆ Using substandard lipsticks can darken the lips. To lighten the colour of dark lips, apply a mixture of honey and limejuice over the lips for a few days.

◆ Winter can rob the skin of its moisture and have a drying effect on it. For a smooth and soft complexion during winter months, apply a mixture of fresh cream and honey on your face and neck.

◆ Remember the good old oil baths, which our grandmothers used to advice. The benefits of oil bath are many. Add four pieces of camphor in 100 ml coconut oil and apply it on your body before bathing, for a smooth and shiny skin.

◆ For dry skin, apply a mixture of glycerine, fresh cream and honey. It will keep the complexion glowing. This is a good treatment for cracked heels, too.

◆ Every woman is terrified of wrinkles. To keep wrinkles at bay, apply a mixture of curd and gram flour to the face and leave it on for 15 minutes before washing it off.

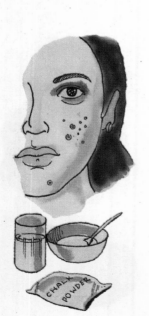

◆ Extract some cabbage juice and mix it with a little yeast and one tablespoon of honey. Apply this mixture on the face and wash after about 20 minutes with lukewarm water. This pack helps in combating dry skin and wrinkle formation.

◆ For instant cure of pimples, apply a paste of chalk and water on them. They will disappear by evening.

◆ For a quick relief from freckles, grate half a white radish; mix with 2 teaspoons of limejuice and tomato juice. Apply on the face and keep it on for 20 minutes. Wash it off with lukewarm water. A regular application will ensure a freckle free face for you.

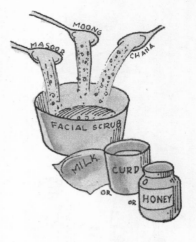

◆ Face scrubs are very helpful in rejuvenating the complexion. They slough off dead and useless skin cells to make way for fresh and new ones. Make a great scrub at home by grinding equal quantities of *chana, moong* and *masoor dals* and mix with milk or curd or honey.

◆ Glycerine mixed with rose water and limejuice is the best remedy for dry skin. Glycerine retains moisture and the lemon juice cleanses the skin.

◆ For a soft and rosy complexion, grind a few fresh or dry rose petals with a dash of milk or fresh cream. Add a teaspoon of gram flour and a few drops of rose water to it. Apply the mixture liberally all over the face and neck. It will help you in reviving a tired and dull skin.

◆ Getting rid of blackheads is quite easy if you try this remedy. Apply a paste of gram flour and curd on the affected area. When the mixture hardens and dries up, gently scrape off with your fingertips and wash the face.

◆ For an excellent face pack, use grated potatoes and honey.

◆ A mixture of 2 tablespoon each of cucumber and carrot juice, acts as an excellent toner for the skin, during winters.

◆ To tighten skin pores, cover the body with a mixture of 2" piece cucumber, 2-tablespoon mint, ½ teaspoon lemon juice and 2-3 drops of vinegar.

◆ Smear the body with equal quantities of vaseline and glycerine 10 minutes prior to bathing. This prevents the skin from drying.

◆ A pack made by mixing a tablespoon each of coarsely ground '*moong dal*' powder, orange rind and milk prevents the skin from drying in winter.

◆ After using a razor or epilator, cover the skin with a paste of gram flour mixed with turmeric and sandalwood powder, fresh cream, lemon juice and milk. This prevents the ingrowth of hair, delays hair growth and softens the skin.

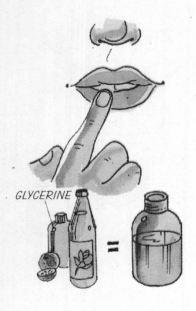

GLYCERINE

◆ For soft lips, apply a mixture of glycerine, limejuice and rose water mixed in equal quantities.

◆ For a glowing skin and lustrous hair, begin your day with a warm glass of water to which a teaspoon of honey has been added. Gorge on fruits for breakfast and salad before lunch and dinner. Have a cupful of curd daily.

◆ For removing blemishes, apply the juice of grated cucumber, potato or watermelon to the face. To remove blackheads, chop a tomato and apply continuously on the affected area.

◆ Use lemon or cucumber juice as astringent. Mix dried orange peel with water. It makes an excellent face scrub. To soften skin, use almonds, curd, turmeric powder or lime juice.

◆ To rejuvenate your face, put papaya pulp on it. To make your face glow, apply fresh orange juice.

◆ To reduce pimples and blackheads, rub the scrapings of bitter gourd on infected portions of the face.

◆ The omnipresent Tulsi plant in many households has a lot of uses. A mixture of finely powdered dry tulsi leaves, 1 tablespoon of milk and almond oil helps clear pimples.

◆ Bananas are not just for eating. They are a very good beauty aid. Mash a ripe banana and mix it with 1-teaspoon honey and a few drops of lemon. This makes an excellent face pack for tired skin.

◆ You don't have to buy expensive hand lotion from the market. You can make one at home by mixing together half-cup rose water, ¼ cup glycerine, ¼ cup aftershave lotion, and ¼ tablespoon white vinegar.

◆ To prevent wrinkles, mix equal proportions of cold cucumber juice with rose water and lemon juice. Cover the region around the eyes with a cotton wool soaked in this mixture.

◆ Don't feel guilty about putting your husband's Vodka bottle to good use. Vodka makes a good pore-tightening astringent cum toner for oily skins.

COTTON WOOL

◆ For a home facial, smear fresh, cold milk (before boiling) on the face for five minutes. Then cover the face with chilled rose water mixed with milk cream. Wash with warm water. Finally cover the face with a pack made from sandalwood and rose water and place slices of cucumber on the eyes. Wash off after 15 minutes.

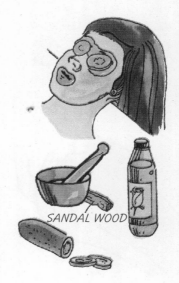

SANDAL WOOD

◆ Never forget to clean your face scrupulously before going to bed. It can work wonders for your complexion. Clean your face of make up residue by scrubbing it with a spoon of gram flour mixed with water.

◆ To remove stretch marks acquired during pregnancy, use ½ teaspoon of aloe, ½ teaspoon papaya pulp, 1-teaspoon rose water, 1 teaspoon sandalwood paste, 10 drops of almond oil and 2 drops of lavender oil. Add 2-teaspoon milk cream to this and make a paste. Apply over the affected skin and massage gently before a bath. Doing this twice a week will take care of the marks.

◆ Mix together 1 cup each of green gram flour and rice flour, ½ cup wheat flour, ¼ cup milk powder, 3 teaspoon turmeric, 4 teaspoon semolina, 2 teaspoon granulated sugar, 4-5 teaspoon red sandalwood powder and 1 teaspoon henna. Mix lemon juice to this mixture and use as a facemask for normal skin.

◆ Mix one teaspoon honey with ½ teaspoon rice powder and rub all over the face, especially on the chin and nose. This removes black as well as white heads.

◆ Rub ice-cold orange juice on dry skin in circular motion. It gives you a glowing complexion.

◆ Bath scrubs give a glowing effect to the body by removing dead skin cells. Make an excellent bath scrub at home by mixing together 1 teaspoon each of sandalwood powder, fuller's earth and dried orange peel powder.

FULLER'S EARTH POWDER

DRIED ORANGE PEEL

SANDAL WOOD

BATH SCRUB.

◆ Mash a few mint leaves, neem leaves and a banana. Apply the paste all over the face and neck, avoiding the eyes. Wash off when dry. This face pack removes scars, freckles and minor skin blemishes.

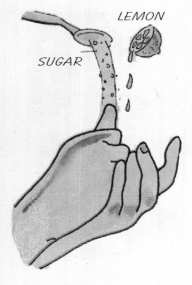

SUGAR

LEMON

- For a very tanned skin, mix the juice of a lemon with sugar, add a little glycerine and scrub gently in circular movements. This will not only get rid of the tan but also soften the skin.

- Rubbing limejuice and sugar between the palms till the sugar dissolves will keep the palms smooth.

- A full body scrub once a week does wonders for the body. Mix 2 teaspoon flour, 1 teaspoon gram flour, a little raw milk, 1 pinch turmeric powder and 1 teaspoon honey for an effective body scrub. One can also use lemon and cream for the body.

- For a glowing skin, mash a banana in a teaspoon of milk and apply the paste on the face.

- Mix equal proportions of vitamin E oil, Vaseline and glycerine. Cover the entire body with this paste and leave it on for an hour. Wash off with cold water for a lovely and soft skin.

- Alpha hydroxy acid (AHA), which is found in citrus fruits, sugarcane and milk that has gone sour, is extremely effective as a natural exfoliant. It can be used to remove dead cells.

- Smoke and dust take their toll on the skin, making it age faster. To retain the skin's natural and youthful look, apply a good anti-wrinkle cream, which contains AHA, vitasomes and special moisturisers, every night.

- Mashed peaches applied on the face brighten and deep cleanse a sallow and dull complexion.

- Add some *neem* or *tulsi* leaves to your hot, bath water, for a soothing and refreshing bath. They take care of minor skin problems and act as disinfectants.

- Applying a paste of sandalwood and rose petals on the face, everyday, will make the skin soft and glowing. Wash off after 10 minutes.

- Smear fresh cream over discoloured lips and leave it on to dry. Use regularly for at least a month to bring back the healthy colour of the lips.

FRESH CREAM

◆ For acne, smear a paste of fresh neem leaves, gram flour, turmeric powder, on the marks and wash off after 20 minutes.

◆ Boil fresh neem leaves in 2 cups of water. Cool, strain and use this liquid as a tonic to reduce pimples.

◆ Wrap ice cubes in a thin cloth and rub lightly all over the face and the neck. This helps in reducing the puffiness around the eyes and the face.

◆ Grate and squeeze out the juice from a tender cucumber. To this add an equal quantity of milk and use over darkened patches of skin. This serves as an excellent whitening tonic.

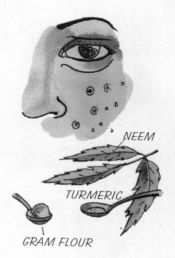

NEEM

TURMERIC

GRAM FLOUR

◆ To get rid of blackheads, cover the area with a mixture of green gram flour, curd and turmeric powder. Leave it for 10 minutes. Scrub off, using cold water.

◆ In a thick-bottomed pan, heat a mixture of egg white and lemon juice till thick. Cool, smear this mixture over the face to get rid of blackheads permanently.

◆ Hairy faces look unattractive. To get rid of facial hair, apply a mixture of fenugreek powder and green gram powder on the unwanted facial hair. Let it dry before scrubbing off.

◆ Mix a tablespoon of rice flour with 2 tablespoons of curd. This is effective cleansing milk, which removes stale make up and opens up the pores.

◆ To get rid of dark circles around the eyes, grind 5 almonds, 1 teaspoon fresh cream, juice of ½ lemon, ½ teaspoon Fuller's earth and ½-grated potato, to a thick paste. Apply it around the eyes. Wipe off with cotton wool dipped in warm milk.

◆ For dull and dark lips, apply the juice of coriander leaves, before going to bed, for 15 days. The effort will pay off when your lips become smooth and attractive once again.

◆ A facemask is a great way of unmasking your beauty. A facemask made by blending egg white and a little lemon juice is an excellent way to prevent wrinkles. Wash off the face pack after 20 minutes with cold water.

CORIANDER JUICE

SALT

CREAM MILK · GLYCERINE

· VITAMIN-E OIL

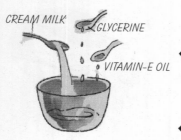

◆ To prevent dry skin during the winters, moisturise it with a mixture of 1" piece of mashed banana, ½ a teaspoon milk cream, 5 drops glycerine and 2 drops of vitamin E oil.

◆ In India, we do not like tanned skin, unlike our western counterparts. To get rid of unwanted tan, mix together equal quantities of olive oil and vinegar. Apply on the affected area, 15 minutes before the bath.

◆ To prevent the effects of sunburn, mix 1-teaspoon potato juice with 1 teaspoon lemon juice and leave it on for 15 minutes. Wash after some time. Repeat for a few days to get rid of the tan.

◆ Rub scraped bitter gourd peels over the face to keep blackheads and pimples at bay. Avoid the areas around the mouth and the eyes.

◆ Beat a raw egg and apply it on the face and neck. Relax for 20 minutes and rinse it off with warm water. Eggs help tighten the skin pores and nourish the skin.

◆ To exfoliate dead cells, rub sugar crystals on the body regularly.

◆ If you are blessed with a normal skin, rub leftover fruits on the face and neck. It keeps the skin nourished and glowing.

◆ A pack made from 3 teaspoon each of cucumber juice, coconut water, lemon juice and sandalwood powder, prevents skin from sagging.

◆ To stop the skin from dehydrating during the winter, minimise the use of soap. Instead, use a mixture of 1 tablespoon each of gram flour and beaten curd, ¼ teaspoon of orange peel powder and 1 teaspoon olive oil.

◆ Don't fret if your milk gets curdled. Just put it to good use. Use the residue of spoilt milk as a moisturiser for dry skin.

◆ Pimples can leave ugly marks on the skin. To remove marks left by pimples, mix radish juice, with equal quantity of buttermilk, apply on face. Wash off after an hour.

BUTTER MILK.

◆ Lips become dry and crack during the winter season. To prevent the lips from getting cracked and chapped, apply crushed fenugreek seeds mixed with milk.

◆ Sponge dry the face with salt and water to prevent it from looking oily and sweaty. This is especially beneficial during the hot summer days when there is a tendency for the skin to excrete more oil than usual.

◆ To remove burn marks from your body, burn a coconut shell and add this ash to coconut oil. Mix well and apply well over the burn marks. They will vanish within some time.

◆ Dried and powdered orange peel mixed with a little gram flour makes an excellent face pack.

◆ To get rid of pigmented skin, mix 1 teaspoon each of lemon juice and honey to papaya pulp. Rub this granular paste on the face and wash off after it dries.

◆ Make a fantastic face-cleanser with 2 cups dried, powdered green peas, 1 cup gram flour, 1 cup dried orange powder and 1 cup of powdered almonds.

◆ Mix equal parts of fresh tomato juice and cucumber juice, add a dash of rose water and refrigerate. It makes an excellent astringent for all types of skin.

◆ While washing the face, add a little powdered sugar to the soap lather. It will help in exfoliating the dead cells from your face.

FENUGREEK

COSMETICS

Although we like to hold on to our cosmetics, especially the ones we buy during our trips abroad or the foreign ones presented by friends; there is an unmentioned expiry date for each cosmetic. Using these cosmetics beyond the expiry date may cause harm to the skin and body. Sometimes one does not quite know when one should get rid of the cosmetics. Here is a quick reckoner, which may help you in deciding which of your lipsticks, creams or lotions should be discarded. It is time to throw away your cosmetics when—

- ◆ Lipstick begins to emanate a strange smell.
- ◆ Creams, lotions and moisturisers become too runny and separate into layers.
- ◆ Liquid mascara hardens up.
- ◆ Compacts harden and cake up.
- ◆ Liquid make-up bottles show a discolouration of the contents.
- ◆ Powder puffs when they become hard and caky.
- ◆ Lipstick brushes when they are no longer soft or the bristles have loosened up.

Lipsticks and nail polishes and hair oils can be stored in the refrigerator to make them last longer.

Old, broken and outdated shades of lipsticks can be re-used. Take 5-6 leftover shades and remove their contents into a small steel bowl with the help of a pointed knife. Heat this on the flame of a candle. Stir the melted product and pour into an empty lipstick container. Keep this in the fridge for half an hour. Shape the point with a knife or use with a lipstick brush.

HAIR

The crowning glory of a woman, the long tresses and shining locks, can be the envy of other women. In these days of pollution and adulteration, it is difficult to retain the luster and thickness of one's hair. As compared to the modern day shampoos, the traditional methods of hair-care can give good results. Here are some tried and tested ways of keeping the tresses healthy.

- ◆ For glowing hair, grind a few whole green grams, lemon peels, a handful of curry leaves and a few 'reethas' to a paste and apply to the hair before washing off.
- ◆ To get rid of nits in the hair, mix equal quantities of vinegar and water and apply on the hair and scalp. Leave for an hour before washing. Brush your hair

backwards with a fine-toothed comb. Doing this for a few days will get rid of the nits.

◆ A few crushed camphor tablets added to hair oil will keep the hair free from lice and infection apart from keeping the scalp cool.

CAMPHOR

◆ For long and healthy hair, wash with tender coconut water.

◆ Add a few drops of eucalyptus oil to the henna mixture before applying to the hair. This will give the hair a rich, coppery colour and get rid of dandruff while leaving it shining.

◆ To prevent hair fall, rub *amla, neem* and fresh coconut milk to the scalp.

◆ Get rid of dandruff with beetroot juice or a mixture of curd, egg and lime. To prevent graying of hair, rub a mixture of curry leaves, *amla* and fresh coconut milk to the scalp.

◆ For soft and silky hair, rinse it with tea decoction to which 1 tablespoon of limejuice has been added.

◆ To give your hair an auburn tinge, boil grated beetroot with ½ teaspoon 'kattha', 1-teaspoon *methi* powder and water. Strain and add it to the henna powder mixed with a teaspoon of coffee powder. Let it stand overnight. In the morning add ½ cup curd to the concoction, mix well and apply to the scalp. Wash off after 3 hours.

◆ To prevent hair loss, dry, powder and mix together each of bay and *neem* leaves and 25 gms of tulsi leaves. Add 5 teaspoons of this mixture to 50 ml water and apply to the scalp once a week.

◆ Dry, powder and mix together lemon peels, rose and hibiscus petals, curry leaves and *shikakai* powder. Mix a tablespoon of this mixture with egg white and use as a conditioner to arrest falling of hair.

◆ Hair conditioners don't come in bottles and jars only. Crushed spinach leaves make an excellent hair conditioner.

◆ Boil ½ cup water with 12 lemon slices in it. When the volume reduces to half, mix in a teaspoon of Vodka and cool. Use this solution to style hair.

RUSTED NAILS

TRIFLA

◆ For a natural hair dye, soak rusted iron nails in water in an iron container. Strain the water, make a paste with *'trifla'* (all spice) powder and apply on the scalp for 2 hours. Wash off with water and you will have shiny, black hair.

◆ To control split ends and treat rough and coarse hair, warm a combination of castor, mustard and olive oil and massage into the scalp for 20 minutes. Steam towel after 2 hours.

◆ Rinse lifeless hair with a solution of 100 ml light tea mixed with ¾ teaspoon vinegar. This helps in adding bounce and .luster to the hair.

◆ If you end up with cold every time you apply henna on your hair, add a few cloves to the henna mixture. The warming properties of cloves will keep you from getting cold.

◆ Massage the contents of a vitamin E capsule into the scalp to revitalise and condition stressed hair. Leave for half an hour and rinse thoroughly.

◆ Many people, especially babies, develop scalp rashes during summers. To prevent summer rashes on the scalp, mix castor, gingerly and coconut oil in equal proportions, leave on the scalp for some time. Wash away with cold water.

◆ Mayonnaise is a good way to add oils to dry hair. Massage it into the hair and wash off after ½ an hour. Do this about twice a month. You get the double benefit of eggs and oil into your hair.

◆ Pluck off a leaf from aloe plant; take the hard green covering off with a knife. The jelly like substance that you get should be mixed with 2-tablespoon vaseline and applied to the hair for moisturing effect.

◆ Once a week, mix a little baking soda with your shampoo, work up a good lather and leave for a minute. This leaves the hair shiny and squeaky-clean.

◆ For rich burgundy sheen to your hair, boil 2-3 teaspoons of tea, 1-teaspoon coffee, a small piece of 'kattha' powder and red sandalwood, in water. Mix this red water with henna powder, add 2 teaspoon of mustard oil and 1 teaspoon of eucalyptus oil (optional). Apply this to the hair for at least 2 hours and then wash.

◆ For a lovely black sheen to the hair, boil 8-10 pieces of *amla*, 2-3 pieces of *shikakai*, 25 gm *harar*, and 25 gm *bahera* and soak overnight, in an iron vessel. Sieve the water and mix henna powder. Apply for 2 hours and then wash it off.

◆ For an emergency henna of hair, sprinkle a little brown powder blush-on and apply on the hair. The hennaed effect will last till the next shampoo.

◆ To stimulate hair follicles, take 2 teaspoon fenugreek seeds, grind and add to the henna mix. The *methi* seeds can also be mixed with curd and applied, to prevent dandruff.

◆ If you don't have the time to wash and dry your hair, sprinkle talcum powder on it and brush vigorously. The powder soaks the excess oil and leaves the hair dry and fluffy.

◆ Massage the paste of 1 tablespoon fenugreek seeds, 1 teaspoon black pepper powder and ½ cup milk gently into the scalp, to get rid of dandruff.

◆ Boil a handful of curry leaves in 100 ml coconut oil and massage this oil into the scalp, twice a week. This prevents loss of hair.

◆ Remember the time when we used to stick chewing gums in each other's hair, in school. Your child may also have been coming back from school with chewing gum stuck in the hair and you may be at your wit's end trying to dislodge the same without pulling out all your child's hair. To remove chewing gum from the hair, rub a little honey over it.

ALMOND OIL

HONEY

◆ To get rid of split ends in the hair, mix together 1 tablespoon of almond oil, 1 teaspoon of honey, 1 egg yolk and smear all over the scalp. Leave it on for about 30 minutes. Wash off with lukewarm water.

◆ Lice and nits are a big nuisance. Every mother has to face the problem of finding her child's hair infested with them at some time or the other. Lice can be removed from the hair by wrapping the hair in a towel full of basil leaves and leaving it overnight. Do it for a week.

TEETH

Even if the smile is beautiful, it can be marred by a set of bad teeth. The art of keeping those pearlies shining is to abide by certain rules.

◆ Sprinkle a little salt on the toothpaste while brushing the teeth to make them sparkle.

◆ Eating a small piece of carrot after meals will clean your mouth of the food particles.

◆ For sparkling teeth, rub them with bay leaf once or twice a week.

◆ Add a drop of clove oil to the toothpaste before brushing your teeth to remove stains on them.

◆ For a home made mouthwash, boil guava leaves in water for ten minutes. Cool, strain and use as mouthwash.

◆ For shining white teeth, take dry lemon peel and powder it. Add a little bit of salt and 2-3 drops of mustard oil. Mix well and use this to clean your teeth. It keeps the bad breath away, too.

HERBAL TREATMENTS

Our scriptures and old manuscripts have records of many remedies, which can take care of almost all types of problems. Be it beauty, health or fitness, there are traditional methods of care for every ailment.

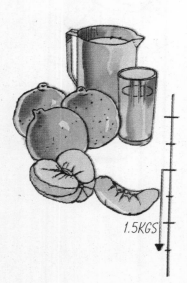

1.5KGS

◆ One whole day on any one variety of fruit and lots of water can help you lose up to 1.5 kgs., besides being very good for the system.

◆ For dull and tired eyes, put grated or sliced cucumber on the eyes while lying down with the curtains drawn.

◆ To prevent lips from darkening due to overuse of lipstick, smear with a pack made from ground almonds, fresh cream and lemon juice.

◆ Roast an onion and make a paste. Use this on the cracks on your feet. The cracks will disappear within a month's time.

◆ To tone delicate eye muscles, reduce black circles and eye pouches, cover the eye sockets with a chilled concoction of egg albumin, lemon, whipped cream and the juices of grated potato and cucumber. Leave for 20 minutes and wash off using cold milk.

◆ For strong and healthy nails, eat jelly and dip nails in gelatine for 5 minutes. Also eat calcium, milk, curd and green salads.

◆ Soak rough and scaly hands in a bowl of warm water to which 1 teaspoon of cornstarch has been added. This regular 5-minute treatment will soften the hands.

◆ Dry your nails in the cold air of the freezer compartment of the refrigerator as soon as you apply nail varnish. It will not chip off easily and will last longer.

◆ Apply some petroleum jelly on your nails if you are about to do a messy job. It will prevent the dirt from getting lodged.

◆ After a bath, massage the feet with a few drops of mustard oil for 5 minutes. Pour 2 mugs of water over them. A daily treatment will make your feet soft.

◆ To soften tough calluses on soles of feet, coat with a mixture of 6 crushed aspirin tablets and half cup each of water and lemon juice. Wrap feet with a warm towel and scrub the calluses with pumice stone after ten minutes. Within a few days the calluses will soften and can be easily removed.

◆ For a quick pedicure, add a few drops of vinegar to ¼ cup curd and rub this mixture well on the feet, ankles, heels and between the toes. After 10 minutes, wash off with warm water. This removes dead tissues and the skin becomes softer, too.

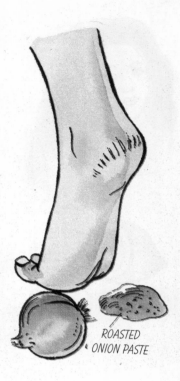

ROASTED ONION PASTE

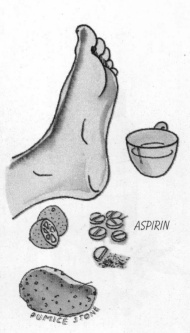

ASPIRIN

PUMICE STONE

♦ Apply a paste made of 2 tablespoon of heated mustard oil and 15 gms wax, leave overnight on cracked heels. The cracks will vanish.

♦ For cracked heels, apply candle wax and mustard oil mixed together in equal ratio and wear a pair of old socks to cover your feet. Do this regularly in order to gain smooth and beautiful feet.

HERBAL HAIR OILS

Any of the following can be used to make herbal oils with base oils such as coconut, mustard oil, castor oil, olive oil, etc. Sometimes two of them can be mixed to make the herbal oil. Hair massage can be done with these hair oils with a touch of water or a drop of lemon juice.

Bhringraj–is also known as '*maka*'. The fragrant leaves of this plant are very useful as they can be used to make very beneficial herbal oil, which has a strong cooling property. This oil helps the hair to grow and also refreshes the eyes. Since it cools the scalp, this oil can be used for curing headaches.

Jabakusum–the common hibiscus is a great source of hair oil with excellent properties. The leaves as well as the flowers of this plant are used to darken greying hair and the oil made out of it helps in hair growth as well as the health of hair.

Neem–ever since the western countries applied for patents of neem products, we have woken up to the benefits of this plant. Oils made out of these leaves and the berries cure headaches, baldness, increase hair growth and strength.

Brahmi–it is a herb, which grows wild everywhere in India. It is the commonest ingredient in hair oils. It cools the head, removes stress and helps hair growth.

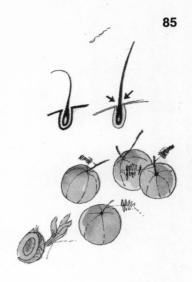

Parijat–also called '*harsingar*', this tree has orange, white, fragrant flowers. The juice of these flowers cures dandruff and strengthens hair roots.

Tulsi–the leaves of this plant when used in oil add lustre to hair.

Castor seeds–hair oil made of these seeds brings about sound sleep and healthy hair.

Curry leaves–also called '*meethi neem*', the leaves when eaten regularly prevent greying. They nourish the roots and restore normal pigmentation of the hair. The leaves can be eaten raw in chutney or their juice may be added to buttermilk or yogurt.

Henna–henna leaves are used to darken the grey hair. They nourish and condition the hair.

Amla–enriches hair growth and pigmentation. Amla water makes a good rinse for the hair.

Health

The modern day men as well as women have become health conscious as well as fitness conscious. They are much more aware about the ills of being physically unfit than the previous generations. One of the reasons could be that the present generation cannot afford to be sick or infirm. They have to be on their feet and active, at all times, till a very late stage in life. People do not have the time to spend worrying about their sickness. The only alternative is to keep oneself fit for action. There is also a growing awareness about the alternative medicines. A large number of people are moving towards different schools of treatment. The alternative therapies are affordable, easily available and effective.

HOME REMEDIES

Long before the western world began formulating the allopathic medicine, our sages and physicians like Charaka and Sushruta, were formulating remedies for almost all ailments. After decades of using the allopathic medicines, people have suddenly begun practising alternative therapies, massages, Reiki, yogic therapies etc. All of a sudden, grandma's traditional treatments have come into demand. These treatments and remedies are neither harmful nor have any side effects like the allopathic medicines. Hence they are inexpensive, effective and safe.

◆ Grind 6-8 'Tulsi' leaves with 2 black peppercorns and have it with honey to treat a fever or a cold. This is one of the most effective treatments for cold and cough.

◆ Drinking wheat grass juice works wonders for diabetics. In fact, many doctors have begun recommending this treatment to their patients, along with the other medications.

◆ To dislodge a wood splinter that has got embedded in your skin, put a few drops of iodine on the affected skin. The piece will turn black, making it easy for you to remove it.

◆ If you have the nagging problem of bad breath, drink at least 5 glasses of water first thing in the morning. This is an instant remedy for bad breath, it also benefits your system by keeping it clean.

◆ Stuffy and blocked nasal passages can be quite awful. To clear a stuffy nose, put a drop of mustard oil in them.

◆ For instant relief from cough, take a pinch of mixture of '*kattha*', cumin seeds and '*misri*', mixed in a 2:1:1 proportion.

◆ Many children suffer from the problem of bedwetting up to a late age. To solve the bedwetting problem of your child, give her a small piece of jaggery to suck at bedtime.

◆ To cure a nagging cough in children, extract the juices of betel leaves and basil leaves. Take 2-3 drops of this mixture and add a little honey to it. It will give immediate relief.

◆ A teaspoon of a mixture of poppy seeds and crystal sugar will help control diarrhoea.

◆ 1 teaspoon castor oil taken with lukewarm water early in the morning on an empty stomach is an excellent cure for indigestion. It also helps in alleviating muscular pain and nervous problems.

◆ Taking a small quantity of warm, boiled rice wrapped in a clean cloth and fomenting the area with it can treat styes.

◆ For relief from inflamed tonsils, apply a mixture of 1-teaspoon 'chuna' and 1 teaspoon ginger juice on the throat.

CHUNA
GINGER JUICE

◆ Dry roast 1 teaspoon each of cummin seeds and caraway seeds (*ajwain*) in a pan. Add 1-cup water and boil till it is reduced to half the quantity. Strain and add sugar to taste. Drinking 1 teaspoon of this will provide relief from acidity and indigestion.

◆ Add a pinch of asafoetida to some lukewarm water and drink it, for relief from menstrual cramps.

◆ Heat 2-3 chillies in cooking oil. Smear this oil on the forehead whenever you suffer from headache.

◆ Grind a lemon along with the seeds and rind to a paste. Add a little salt. This makes an effective cure for diarrhoea.

◆ To relieve toothache, boil a few guava leaves in water. Strain the water and gargle with the extract. Repeat several times and the toothache will disappear.

◆ Eating a ripe papaya with a pinch of cummin powder, pepper and salt cures constipation and indigestion.

◆ Adding a teaspoon of castor oil while kneading the 'atta' takes care of the constipation problem.

◆ Half a teaspoon of ginger paste applied on the forehead helps in getting rid of a headache.

◆ To get rid of an earache, place a little asafoetida wrapped in a small piece of cloth in the ear.

◆ Do you repel people due to bad breath? Here is a helpful hint. To get rid of bad breath caused by onion eating, eat a few coriander seeds.

◆ In fact, there are a number of ways by which you can ensure that your breath remains fresh. Take 2 tbsp of grated fresh, ginger and 1½ tbsp of jaggery. Chew this mixture and your bad breath will disappear.

◆ For getting rid of irritating ulcers on the tongue, apply a little paste of coriander leaves.

◆ To find relief from severe menstrual cramps, peel a few garlic flakes, fry them in ghee, cool, add sugar and swallow a couple of them. You will get relief in ten minutes.

◆ For instant relief from cold, add ½ teaspoon turmeric powder to a glass of hot milk and drink it.

◆ To get rid of a bad cold, chop some cabbage and put it in boiling water. Inhale the steam at least twice a day.

◆ For instant relief from cough, drink a little hot water with a pinch of salt and ½ teaspoon of turmeric powder.

◆ When the shoe pinches, stick a small piece of sponge on the shoe's inner surface.

◆ Drink a concoction of 1-teaspoon honey dissolved in ½ a glass of lukewarm water. It is an instant pick-me-up.

◆ Deworming frequently keeps the system working perfectly. Drink the juice of fresh mint leaves to cure worms. It helps children tremendously.

BOILED WATER

CABBAGE

◆ For relief from severe cold, mix 1 teaspoon ginger juice, 1-teaspoon betel leaf juice and 2 teaspoon honey. Warm the mixture and sip it 2-3 times a day. Always drink hot water immediately after.

◆ To get a tight ring off your finger, rub hand lotion or baby oil over the finger and gently move the ring back and forth so that some of the cream gets under the ring. The ring will then, slide off easily.

◆ To counter dehydration during chills and fever, drink as much water and juice as possible.

◆ To cure sore throat, gargle with warm salt water ($^1/_4$ teaspoon salt in 8 oz. Water). Keep the throat moist by using a vapouriser and sucking on hard candy or fruit juice ice cubes.

◆ To thin nasal secretion while suffering from stuffy nose, use a room vapouriser. Eat hot and spicy food; drink hot broth and other hot drinks (tea with honey) and refrain from consuming daily products.

◆ Add sugar and water to the juice of coriander leaves and drink it at bedtime to cure insomnia.

CORIANDER

SUGAR

◆ You can make you own nasal spray by adding ¼ teaspoon salt and ¼ teaspoon baking powder to 8 oz.

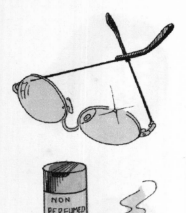

water. The other things that you can do is to take a long, hot shower. Try sleeping on your back with your head raised on two or three pillows.

♦ To add a sparkle to your lenses, clean them with warm water, put a drop of mild, non-perfumed liquid soap and rub with the fingers. Rinse under warm running water and dry with soft, lint-free cloth. However, if the glasses have an anti-reflective coating, clean only with a special solution developed especially for them.

♦ Grind 1 cm. Piece of ginger, 2 cloves, 3 peppercorns and ¼ teaspoon 'saunf' to a fine powder. Add it to the water while making tea. It provides a medicinal value by keeping cold at a bay.

♦ To soothe insect bites, mix 2 tablespoon of olive oil with 1 egg white and apply over the affected area to take away the sting and reduce the swelling. This mix can also be stored in a bottle.

♦ For emergency treatment of a wound, crush tender leaves of the marigold plant and apply the juice along with the crushed leaves on the lining of the band-aid. This will stop the bleeding and also act as a disinfectant.

♦ Most people get a headache when they go out in bright sun, at least I do. To relieve headaches caused by bright sunlight, I drink a mixture of limejuice and ginger paste with warm water. You can try it, too.

♦ For arthritic pain, eat a marble size ball of jaggery coated with 2 teaspoon of amla powder everyday, for about 3 months.

♦ For making home made carminative, make thick syrup with jaggery and add some cut pieces of ginger to it. This mixture is excellent for soothing upset stomachs.

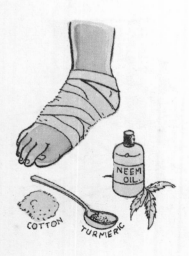

♦ For quick healing of wound, add half a teaspoon of turmeric powder to *neem* oil. Heat it and dip cotton wool in it. Place this on a wound and bandage it.

◆ To treat a persistent cold, warm a spoonful of mustard oil and put a few drops in each nostril.

◆ For immediate relief from aches in legs or hands, immerse the affected limb in hot water mixed with salt.

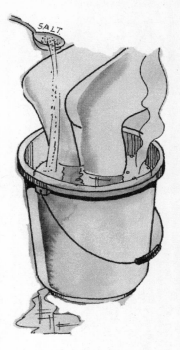

◆ For bruises, dip cotton wool in neat vinegar, bandage the affected area and keep until the dressing is dry. Relief is almost instant.

◆ The white of an egg can be used instead of a burn ointment, during emergency.

◆ Apply a paste of sandalwood powder and milk over prickly heat, for immediate relief.

◆ To control high blood pressure, mix equal quantities of onion juice and honey and take 1 teaspoon every morning.

◆ For curing boils, soak bread in warm milk and sandwich the mixture between the folds of a clean cotton cloth. Apply this poultice to the boil and hold it in place with a cotton bandage. This draws the dirt to the surface of the skin and bursts the boil.

◆ To get rid of an irritating cold, eat a pinch of black pepper in the night.

◆ For stopping diarrhoea, a strong cup of unsweetened black tea is very effective. Another method is to peel an apple and shred it. Keep the shredded pieces in a plate for about 20 minutes until they turn brown in colour. Then eat them.

◆ Eating a few liquorice sticks can cure constipation. It is a natural laxative.

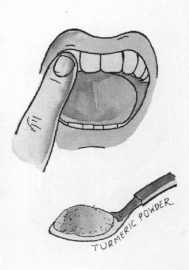

◆ For coughs cut a few pieces of garlic into thin slices. Cover them with honey, leave for 2-3 hours. Drink a spoonful of the resulting juice throughout the day.

◆ When the eyes are red and tired, put a piece of cotton soaked in *jeera* water over them. To make *jeera* water, soak 2 teaspoons of jeera in 10 teaspoons of water, for one hour.

◆ For instant relief from toothache, press a little turmeric powder into the tooth.

◆ To cure a persistent cough, bake a guava in an oven or over charcoal and eat it for four to five days.

◆ Apply ice on hurts, bee stings or burns immediately. The numbing sensation will kill pain and there will be no swelling either.

◆ For bleeding gums, gargle with warm water to which ½ teaspoon of salt has been added. Do it regularly after brushing your teeth.

◆ Honey is good for treating burns. Spread a thin layer over the burnt area; repeat it after every 2-3 hours. The natural gel contained in aloe-vera is also a good soother for burns.

◆ For sprains, chop raw onions and put them in a towel. Put them over the sprain to relieve the pain and reduce the swelling. Alternatively, make a footbath of lavender oil and water, and soak the ankle.

◆ Rub the inner surface of leather shoes with a piece of raw potato to prevent blisters on feet.

◆ Asthma, cough spasms, nausea and vomiting can be temporarily controlled by drinking ½ a cup of fresh onion juice with 2 teaspoons of honey.

◆ Burns will dry within a day or two if smeared with a little coconut oil every half an hour.

◆ To stop bleeding of gums after a tooth extraction, press a cool, moist tea bag against them, with your finger. Hold it in position till bleeding stops.

◆ Boil a handful of cloves and a few pieces of the bark of a neem tree, in half a litre of water for 20 minutes. Cool, strain and refrigerate. This concentrate smeared on an aching tooth relieves pain, instantly.

◆ Smelly feet? Ugh! Soaking them in strong tea for 20 minutes can control smelly feet. Brew 2 tea bags in 500 ml for 15 minutes and pour the tea into a basin contain 2 litres of cool water.

◆ Soaking feet for about 10 minutes in a footbath of apple cider vinegar mixed with water will soothe the cracked heels.

◆ To lose weight drink a glassful of lukewarm water to which 1-teaspoon honey and a few drops lemon juice have been added.

◆ Oil in which fish has been fried should be smeared over aching joints. This remedy gives instant relief.

◆ To cure headaches, use the Chinese acupressure technique. Place your thumb on the web of the skin between the thumb and the index finger of your other palm and apply pressure for about 2 minutes. Repeat on the other hand. Pregnant women should not do this.

◆ Insomniacs can eat a teaspoon of cumin powder mixed with the pulp of a banana, to induce sleep at night.

◆ Dabbing the inside of the nostril with a cotton bud dipped in rose water can halt nosebleeds.

◆ To get rid of acidity; drink a glass of milk to which a pinch of soda bicarb has been added.

◆ Munch on a small piece of ginger after eating raw onion or garlic. It acts as a good mouth freshener.

◆ Rub an aspirin on a bee sting, to stop pain.

◆ During summers, some people experience pain and burning sensation while urinating. This is mainly due to the fact that they drink very little water during the day. Eating rice gruel with 1 teaspoon of butter or gingelly oil will be helpful in easing the pain.

◆ To get rid of boils on scalp, apply coconut oil mixed with camphor.

◆ For bleeding gums, boil some guava leaves in water. Gargle with this 3-4 times a day.

◆ For getting rid of blisters on the tongue, apply ground green coriander leaves.

◆ For earache, apply a mixture of clove and ghee.

◆ To keep blood pressure under control, take 1 teaspoon of fenugreek seed powder with half a glass of water, every morning.

FENUGREEK

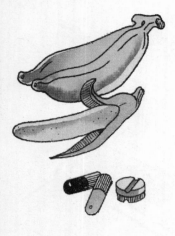

◆ Eating a banana while swallowing a capsule helps it go down easily. This is especially useful when administering capsules to small children.

◆ To get relief from a cold, drink a mixture of 2-teaspoon honey, 1 teaspoon ginger juice and 1-teaspoon betel juice and follow it up with some warm water. Repeating this for 3 times a day will cure the cold fast.

◆ One teaspoon of mint juice mixed with an equal amount of honey and lemon juice is a good cure for indigestion.

◆ One cooked banana flower eaten with curd is a good cure for excessive bleeding during menstruation.

◆ To stop spectacles from slipping over the bridge of the nose, roll some deodorant on the nose.

◆ Honey is an excellent antiseptic and stops bleeding from wounds or cuts when applied locally.

◆ To remove a foreign particle from your eye, fill a glass with water to the brim, place your eye in it and rotate the eyeball.

◆ Wearing spectacles while cleaning fans or ceiling will prevent the dust from falling into the eyes.

DIGESTIVE DISORDERS — CAUSES AND REMEDIES

With the growing pollution, sedentary lifestyle, adulteration in food, wrong food habits and unsafe drinking water, more and more people are succumbing to digestive disorders ranging from heartburn to ulcers. Since digestion is one of the most important systems of the human body, any flaw in the smooth running of this system can cause a variety of problems, which may manifest themselves in various ways. It is, therefore, important to understand the causes and know the remedies, too. Eating the wrong types of food can also cause digestive disturbances.

Flatulence–food that produce gas are raw cucumbers, cabbage, peas, tomatoes, peanuts, raisins, mango, rice, potatoes, milk etc.

Remedies–

- Take a glass of orange juice at breakfast.

- Drink some warm water after a glass of apple juice.

- Include papayas in breakfast or dinner.

- Apply and massage mustard oil around and above the navel.

- Chew aniseeds (*saunf*) soaked in lemon juice, after each meal.

- Take one teaspoon of *ajwain* powder mixed with a pinch of black salt added to a glass of dilute buttermilk, twice daily.

Heartburn

- Take a bland diet consisting of salads and lots of vegetables.

- Avoid pungent, spicy and fatty food.

- Take juice of one lemon in a glass of tomato juice mixed with a spoon of honey, twice a day.

Hyperacidity

- Include milk, butter, fruits like bananas and mangoes, boiled vegetables, dates and milk extracted from almonds. Avoid all citrus fruits and raw vegetables.

- Take milk without cream, in moderate quantities, three times a day.

- Instead of three big meals, take four to five small ones.

- Avoid overeating or drinking water in between the meals.

- Chew food thoroughly. Avoid too hot or cold foods.

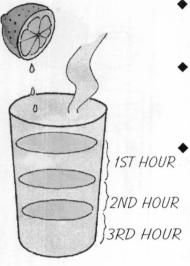

1ST HOUR

2ND HOUR

3RD HOUR

◆ Do not eat when upset or tense or nagged by worry. Have a calm and peaceful attitude towards everything.

◆ Add the juice of a lemon, to a glass of warm water and divide into 3 portions. Take every one-hour in the evening for a few days at a stretch. Sip slowly, do not gulp.

◆ To avoid acidity, take only buttermilk for a week. This will serve as an alkaline cleanser and neutraliser of the acidic state of the system. After this stomach wash, take a well balanced diet with a pre-dominance of raw foods and plenty of fruits and juices to flush out the acidic residues. Juices of citrus fruits are especially beneficial.

◆ Bananas are very good for neutralising the acidity of the body juices and the mucilage in them coats the lining of the stomach.

◆ Raw cabbage and cabbage juices mixed with carrot juice, not only neutralises the excessive acid, but also regenerates the frayed mucosal lining of the stomach and the intestines.

THE BENEFITS OF FRUITS AND VEGETABLE JUICES

Fruits and vegetables are a veritable treasure-mine of valuable nutrients. Some improve eyesight, some strengthen bones and teeth, some are good for the digestive system and yet others have medicinal value. Fruits and vegetable juices and tender coconut water are very rich in vitamins and minerals, and can work wonders on the health of a person. Simple juices with a touch of spice or flavour, can give a fitness fiend not only nutrition but also a glowing and energetic appearance.

Apple–This fruit can be used for no less than nine ailments.

1. **For constipation**–take at least 2 apples daily.
2. **For diarrhoea**–take 2 cooked apples a day.
3. **For dysentery** (especially for children)–make a paste of a ripe apple and give 1 tablespoon several times a day.
4. **For headache**–take an apple with a little salt, every morning for a week.
5. **For heart problems**–take an apple with honey, once a day.
6. **For rheumatism, gout**–include an apple in your diet.
7. **For eye disorders**–take a few apple peels. Pour enough water to cover the peels and boil them for a few minutes. Strain the water and add a little honey. This can be taken internally. The water can also be used as an eye wash.

Custard Apple

The parts used are the leaf, fruit, bark, roots and seeds.

1. **For tumor**–apply the paste of an unripe custard apple with salt.
2. **For anemia and weaknesses**–take 200 ml of juice (morning before meals, and evening before going to bed).
3. **For ulcers and carbuncles**–make a paste of the leaves and apply.
4. **For hysteria, fits, and fainting**–crush a few leaves and sniff them.
5. **For a hair wash**–use the seed powder mixed with the powder of gram.

Jackfruit

The parts used are the leaves and the fruit.

1. **For glandular swelling, abscess and boils**–apply the milky juice of the plant alone or with vinegar.

2. **For diabetes**–take a decoction of the leaf stalk. Dose–120 ml once a day.

3. **As a tonic**–this tonic is especially good for tuberculosis. Take the 'Koa' (edible portion) of a half ripe jackfruit. Take a clean glass container and put the Koa and jaggery in alternate layers (1:1). Cover the container and leave in the sun for 21 days. Dose–1 tablespoon twice a day.

Guava

For diarrhoea–boil a handful of tender leaves in 4 glasses of water and reduce to 1 glass. Dose–120 ml thrice a day.

For cholera–dry fry 1 tablespoon guava buds (cut into small pieces) with 1 tablespoon black pepper. Crush them, boil the powder in a glass of water and reduce it to half. Give 1-2 tablespoons every hour. Good for diarrhoea also.

For scabies–boil a handful of leaves and wash the body with the water.

For constipation, piles–eat a ripe fruit before meals, for a few days.

Papaya

For intestinal worms–make a paste of 7 mature seeds; take it with hot water at bedtime for 3 days. Take another course after 15 days.

For constipation–eat the ripe fruit at regular intervals.

For amenorrhoea–take a teaspoon of the milky juice of the fruit with sugar candy, twice a day, for 7 days before menstruation.

For ulcer, infected wound–apply the paste of an unripe fruit.

For psoriasis and eczema–apply the milky juice of the fruit.

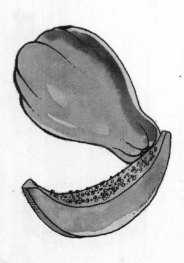

Banana

For anemia, weakness–beat 2 ripe bananas and 1 cup curd together, add sugar to taste and take it in the morning or noon, for 15-21 days.

For diarrhoea, ulcer, and kidney stone–take the stem juice. Dose–100 ml with equal amount of water, at frequent intervals.

For nausea, vomiting–take the juice of the stem with a little honey. Dose–75 ml.

For burns–apply the juice of the stem with ghee.

Mango

For diarrhoea, dysentery–take 1 tablespoon of seed kernel powder, with buttermilk or cold water, 2-3 times a day.

For heat exhaustion–cook an unripe mango. Make an infusion; drink the cool sherbet at frequent intervals. Apply the pulp and bathe after 15 minutes.

For diabetes, scurvy–eat a few tender leaves regularly or take 1 teaspoon of the juice of tender leaves twice a day.

For pyorrhoea, gum problems–mix the fine powder of mango leaves, *brahmi* and *pudina* (4:2:1). To this add a little pepper powder, dry ginger powder, nutmeg powder, clove powder, salt and charcoal. Use the powder as a toothpowder.

For jaundice–juice of root bark, trunk bark. Dose–2 teaspoon with water, thrice a day for 3-5 days. (See Annexure-3).

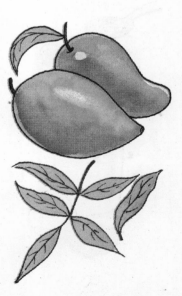

Fruit Juices

Although one always hears of the benefits of fruits and fruit juices, not everyone is fully informed about the specific advantages of the fruit juices. Here are some interesting facts—

Fruits can be broadly classified into three sections.

1. **Acidic fruits**–oranges, limes, lemons, grapefruits, pineapples, tamarind.

2. **Sub-acidic fruits**–apples, pears, apricots, berries, guavas, cherries, grapes, peaches, plums and practically all deciduous fruits.

3. **Sweet fruits**–dates, figs, sweet grapes, raisins, bananas, papaya, chikoo, custard apple, jackfruit.

Apple Juice–It purifies the blood stream if taken early in the morning. It also improves appetite and prevents intestinal infections.

Orange Juice–It prevents and cures scurvy. It aborts a developing cold if taken immediately at the onset of a common cold. When taken in quantities, it is an excellent blood cleanser due to its speedy effect on the acidic condition of the body.

Pineapple Juice–It helps in digesting proteins. It is good for people suffering from sore throat, tonsillitis, colds and digestive upsets. It is also good as a diet supplement to individuals on a strict diet.

Lemon Juice–It is the king of all juices. A rich source of vitamin C, it is also a good laxative. Lemon juice, mixed with honey, is good for weight reduction, influenza, sore throat, cough, colds etc. People suffering from hyperacidity should not drink it in excess. It has good cosmetic qualities as it softens and improves the complexion and is excellent for removing corns and calluses.

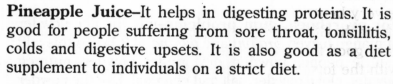

HONEY

Vegetable Juices

If one is not able to find fruits or cannot afford to have fruit juices, regularly, there is no need to despair. Vegetable juices are equally effective and affordable, too. Even the low cost carrot or tomato juice can provide the necessary elements required for good health.

The juices taken from vegetables should preferably be drunk before a meal.

Onion Juice–Onion is a blood purifier. It should be drunk in combination with other juices like carrot juice, beetroot juice etc. Onion juice removes blemishes of the skin and also prevents hair loss. For clearing up skin blemishes, juices can also be applied on the skin.

Carrot Juice–It is a very powerful acid neutraliser, a system cleanser and a blood purifier. It is very good for the eyes, for respiratory problems and for expectant mothers. Carrot juice has also been found to have strong anti-cancer properties. Carrots and celery juices being rich in minerals also have an effective alkaline reaction and are useful in counteracting acidity.

Beetroot Juice–It is a very good blood purifier and is very beneficial for the disorders of the skin and the stomach. Good in counteracting constipation. It is also very good for anaemic patients as it enriches the blood with the formation of red blood corpuscles.

Cucumber Juice–It stimulates the flow of urine and expels noxious waste products (toxins) produced by the body. It is also good for patients suffering from high blood pressure or overweight and is recommended for local application to remove skin blemishes and to reduce the oiliness of the skin.

Tomato Juice–It reactivates a sluggish liver. In fact, it is good for nearly all problems related to liver, digestion and skin. (See Annexure-3).

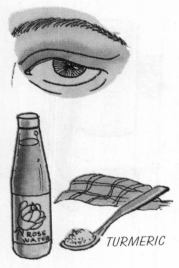

TURMERIC

FLOWER POWER

Flowers have been known to help in curing of certain ailments. They are easily available and affordable. They also have the advantage of giving no side effects while curing many physical ailments. Lately, flower power has gained a lot of attention because of the curative nature of aromatherapy.

◆ To cure uterine problems, make a mixture of rose petals and jaggery (1:1) and sun it for 21 days. Pour the juice in a container and preserve. Taking this concoction thrice a day will relieve most uterine problems.

◆ To cure conjunctivitis, add ½ teaspoon of turmeric powder to some rose water. Strain it through a fine cloth and use this as eye drops. This solution should not be kept for more than two weeks.

◆ To cure constipation and gas troubles, 10-15 rose petals should be eaten every day.

◆ The shoe flower (hibiscus) can be used to cure boils or carbuncles. Crush sufficient amount of fresh leaves or flower buds and apply directly as a poultice over the affected area.

◆ After mumps, boil 30 gm of fresh marigold leaves or flowers in 300 ml water. Decoct it to 150 ml. Divide the concoction into 2 parts. Drink one part in the morning and the other in the evening.

◆ The root stalk (fresh or sun dried) of canna can be used to cure acute infectious hepatitis. Boil 60-120 gms and divide the decoction into 2 parts, to be taken in the morning and evening. The decoction should not be re-heated. The medicine should be taken for 20-30 days.

◆ The cock's comb can be used to treat uterine bleeding, bleeding piles, dysentery and vomiting of blood. For functional uterine bleeding, oven dry or toast 250 gms of sun dried inflorescence. Pulverize finely. Take 6 gms of this powder with water, twice

PERIWINKLE

daily. For bleeding piles, use only 120 gms of the flower. For dysentery and vomiting of blood, boil 6-12 gms of the dried inflorescence in water and drink the decoction.

◆ Diabetics will benefit from eating 4 flowers of white periwinkles daily in the morning. Alternatively, boil them in ½ cup water and decoct to ¼ cup and drink this every morning on empty stomach.

◆ For diarrhoea and dysentery, boil 30 leaves of periwinkle in 250 ml water. Decoct it to 125 ml and drink equal parts of this solution during morning and evening for 5 days.

◆ Prickly lantana leaves can be boiled and the decoction used for washing the affected area, in case of skin ailments like eczema, dermatitis, puritis and furuncles.

◆ Periwinkle flowers can be used for burns and scalds too. Pound sufficient amount of fresh leaves and add some rice flour. Use as a covering for the affected part.

◆ To cure constipation, boil 6-9 gms of periwinkle roots in 1 glass of water. Reduce to ¼ cup and drink it before going to bed.

BROWN SUGAR.
· DRIED MARIGOLD

◆ Big marigold can be used to cure upper respiratory tract infection, cough, bronchitis, pharyngitis, toothache, conjunctivitis, irregular menstruation, and dysmenorrhea. Boil 9-15 gm of dried flowers in 150 ml water. Decoct to 75 ml and divide it into 2 parts. Drink one part in the morning and the other in the evening.

◆ For whooping cough, boil 15 pieces of dried marigold flowers in sufficient amount of water. Add brown sugar and make syrup. Drink this syrup in two divided doses, daily.

SLEEPING TIPS FOR INSOMNIACS

◆ A hot and cold glass of milk promotes sleep. Tryptophan, which contains amino acid, helps induce sleep.

◆ Do not watch violent movies or read thriller before going to bed.

◆ A shower before going to bed also helps as it relaxes and soothes the nerves.

◆ Practice deep relaxation techniques like deep breathing, meditation, yoga, massage etc. These help by reducing the stress factors.

◆ Quit smoking. At least don't smoke before going to bed.

◆ Avoid rich food in your dinner. Large and heavy meals within an hour or two of bedtime cause disturbed sleep.

◆ Reduce the intake of stimulants like coffee, tea, chocolates and drugs that contain stimulants. Don't drink coffee or take alcohol after evening.

◆ Deficiencies in vitamin B, calcium, copper, iron or magnesium can cause sleeping disorders.

◆ Listen to soothing music, preferably instrumental music.

◆ Don't get into arguments or tense discussions after dinner.

◆ Say your prayers and try to relax.

STRESS MANAGEMENT TIPS

No book, which deals with a chapter on health, can be complete without dealing with the problems of stress. Stress has been identified as the greatest killer of this century. It has been found to be the cause of all types of illnesses, coronary problems, digestive disorders, heart problems and even diabetes. But, the present style of living hardly allows anyone to

keep away from stress. The cut throat competition in working life, consumerism and a lust for more, are the deep malaise causing factors. But one can try to control the stress factors to a large extent. With constant effort, stress can be controlled and kept in check.

How does one know that one is tense? There are several emotional reactions to stress, such as—

◆ There is a feeling of conflict, frustration and aggression.

◆ A feeling of tension and inability to relax.

◆ Subjective awareness of being under pressure.

◆ Feeling mentally and physically exhausted without having put in much work.

◆ Increased incidents of indecision. Reduced efficiency.

◆ Restlessness, sleeplessness, increased tearfulness.

◆ Inability to cope with situations and lack of ability to feel pleasure or enjoyment.

◆ Becoming more fussy, pessimistic, gloomy or depressed.

◆ Facing an urge to run and hide.

The physical reactions to stress will bring—

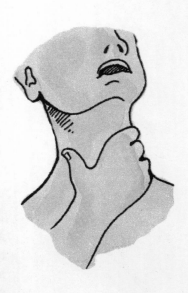

◆ A constant headache.

◆ Insomnia

◆ Rapid, erratic or more pronounced heart beat.

◆ Dryness of mouth and throat.

◆ Backache and breathlessness.

◆ Frequent urge to pass urine.

◆ Profuse sweating.

◆ Chest discomfort.

◆ Change in appetite.

◆ Nausea and squeamishness.

◆ A constant feeling of exhaustion and weakness.

Stress Busters

◆ Regular exercise—any form of exercise, be it walking, skipping, swimming, playing any game, will help you relieve stress.

◆ Take up hobbies and interests—have something to do besides your profession.

◆ Music—music is one of the best remedies to reduce stress. Listen to soft and soothing music or better still, start playing some instrument.

◆ Get to know yourself better—understand your limitations. No one is a super human. Everyone makes mistakes and there are limits to his capability. Accept this truth and flow with it.

◆ Don't bottle up your emotions. Letting your anger out or bursting into tears is a method by which you can let out your steam.

◆ Always get your priorities right. Don't try to achieve too many things at the same time.

◆ Eat good, wholesome food and lead a regular life style.

◆ Take frequent breaks from work. Go on a vacation at least once a year. Get away from the city and try out the small towns or hills. Seas have a calming effect, too.

◆ Learn to laugh if you have forgotten to do so. Let the child in you surface. Laugh at yourself and watch the effect. Laughter is always the best medicine.

◆ Get religious. Religion is one of the best healers and stress busters. Meditation is the ultimate. Practise yoga and meditation.

Meditation

Meditation is one of those methods, which have proved to be exceptionally effective in bringing down the stress levels. People all over the world are learning to practise meditation and are deriving very good results from it.

Doctors recommend it for people with high incidence of blood pressure and heart problems. A lot of people are unable to take up meditation and do not know how to go about it in a proper manner.

It took me a full year of determination to learn meditation. I was one of those who could never sit still or focus the attention for too long. All types of thoughts would fleet across my mind whenever I tried to sit still with closed eyes. However, I was determined to learn the art and continued to make efforts. Now, I can relax and keep my mind still. And that is what meditation is all about.

Though there are no hard and fast rules there are various forms of meditating. Transcendental meditation, Vipassana and yogic meditation, all lead to the same goal. Although it is best to learn the art from a person who is experienced in it, sometimes it is not possible to do so. Given here are some basic guiding rules to help you meditate. These are taken from the Vipassana technique of meditation.

◆ Start by sitting comfortably in a quiet place with a minimum amount of disturbance.

◆ Close your eyes without tensing them.

◆ Take a deep breath or two and settle down to normal breathing pattern. Breathe normally, naturally and gently, allow your awareness to be on your breathing process. Simply observe your breath, trying not to control it or alter it in any conscious manner.

◆ As you observe your breath, you may notice that it changes on its own accord. It may vary in speed, rhythm, depth and sometimes it may even appear to stop for a time. Whatever happens with your breathing, innocently observe it without trying to cause or initiate any changes.

◆ You will find that your attention drifts away from your breath and you are thinking about other things or listening to noises outside. The mind constantly

wanders, refusing to concentrate. Whenever you notice that you are not observing your breath, gently bring your attention back to your breathing.

◆ If during meditation, you notice that you are focusing on some feeling, mood or expectation, treat it as would treat any thought and bring your attention back to your breathing.

◆ Practise this technique for about fifteen minutes.

◆ At the end of those fifteen minutes, keep your eyes closed and just sit quietly for 2-3 minutes. Allow yourself to come out of the meditation gradually before opening your eyes and resuming your normal activities for the day.

◆ Although no set time has been delineated for meditation, it is best done in the early morning, as there is a minimum distraction at that hour.

◆ Initially it will be difficult to hold the concentration for more than a few seconds and you will find your mind wandering constantly. But don't let that phenomenon instill a sense of defeat. Don't give up. If you continue the effort you will find yourself being able to increase the span of meditation. It is a slow but sure process.

You may find yourself experiencing some strange sensations, which are difficult to pen down. These are normal sensations and they denote that you are able to focus your energies. The general experiences one goes through are—

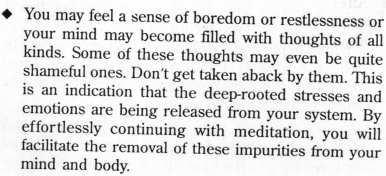

◆ You may feel a sense of boredom or restlessness or your mind may become filled with thoughts of all kinds. Some of these thoughts may even be quite shameful ones. Don't get taken aback by them. This is an indication that the deep-rooted stresses and emotions are being released from your system. By effortlessly continuing with meditation, you will facilitate the removal of these impurities from your mind and body.

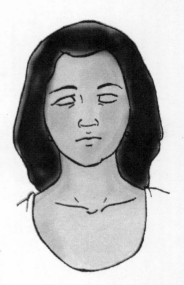

◆ You may even fall asleep. If you fall asleep in meditation, it is an indication that you need more rest during other times of the day. It also means that you have been neglecting the rest phase of your body and not heeding to its signals.

◆ You may slip into the 'gap' when the mantra or breath becomes very settled and refined. You slip into the gap between thoughts, beyond sound, beyond breath. This is also quite a natural process and one need not feel worried about these experiences.

◆ If you stay rested, take care of yourself and take time to commit to meditation. You are bound to get in touch with your inner self. You will tap the cosmic mind, the voice that whispers to you non-verbally in the silent spaces between your thoughts. This is your inner intelligence, and it is the ultimate and supreme genius that mirrors the wisdom of the universe. Trust this inner wisdom and all your efforts will come true.

◆ Success in meditating will give you an uplifting sensation, which is pure joy and bliss. It will make your soul feel light and happy and most bodily ailments like aches and pains will gradually disappear.

◆ You will be able to see the change in yourself and your working. The efficiency will increase and your patience will also increase. The human dealings and relationships will undergo a vast change. There will be a feeling of generosity and an all-pervading sense of joy.

◆ After several months of practising meditation successfully, you will begin to notice a gradual change in your personality.

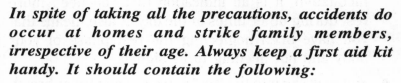

FIRST AID KIT

In spite of taking all the precautions, accidents do occur at homes and strike family members, irrespective of their age. Always keep a first aid kit handy. It should contain the following:

1. A small pair of scissors, a knife and a few safety pins.
2. A roll of sterlised cotton.
3. A few strips of band-aid.
4. A few rolls of gauge.
5. An antiseptic cream.
6. A thermometer.
7. A few medicines like painkillers.
8. Dettol.

Keep it away from the reach of children and replenish your supply of old medicines, which have crossed their expiry date with new ones.

Some Safety Tips About Use of Medicines

1. Always buy medicines manufactured by reputed companies.
2. Buy your medicines from a good retailer.
3. Always make sure of the date of manufacture and the expiry date of the medicines.
4. See that the medicines you buy have the same dosage as per the prescription.
5. Sulpha drugs, antibiotics and sleep-inducing pills should not be taken without a doctor's prescription.
6. Never stock medicines.
7. Throw away the medicines after the expiry date is over.
8. Store the medicines as advised on the label.
9. Never self-medicate.
10. Keep the medicines away from the reach of children.

FIRST AID TIPS

Accidents happen both in the house and outside. Many of these turn fatal because the people around the victim either panic or commit a grave mistake because of lack of knowledge. It is necessary that every person should know a few basic first-aid tips which could provide succour to the victim before the doctor arrives.

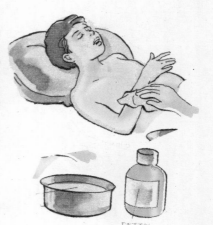

1. Profuse bleeding from a wound

a) Try to stop the bleeding initially or it could lead to harmful consequences.

b) Make the person lie flat on the ground.

c) Take a clean cloth and dip it in ice-cold water, mixed with an antiseptic solution like dettol. Place it over the wound after wringing out the excess water.

d) If the bleeding doesn't stop, put a padded cotton pad over the wound and tie it tightly. Call the doctor immediately.

2. Small cuts

a) Wash the wound with water.

b) Apply tincture iodine or dettol on the wound.

c) Put band-aid, if required.

3. Burns

a) Wash the affected area under running water for a few minutes.

b) Apply burnol on the area after pat drying it.

c) If burnol is not available, apply a concentrated salt solution over the area.

4. Fire

a) If your clothes catch fire, roll on the floor to extinguish the fire or wrap a blanket over you to cut of the supply of air.

b) Clothes stuck to the body should be removed with coconut oil.

c) After every 15-20 minutes, give some water mixed with a little salt to the victim.

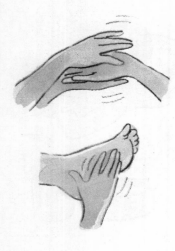

d) Call the doctor immediately.

e) If the fire is caused by a short circuit, switch off the mains and try to drowse the fire with an fire extinguisher, never water.

f) Never use a lift, if fire catches a high-rise building. Use the stairs instead.

g) Always keep the fire extinguisher handy.

h) Call the fire-brigade immediately.

5. Electric shock

a) Switch off the mains before trying to disentangle a person.

b) Always use a wooden stick or rubber gloves while holding a person who has received a shock.

c) Stand on a wooden stool or board or wear dry rubber slippers as an additional precaution.

d) Give the victim some hot coffee/tea or milk to help him recover from the shock. Also keep a hot water bottle near his feet.

e) If the victim faints, try to recover him by massaging his soles and palms and sprinkling some water on the face.

f) Try to give artificial respiration to the victim if required, till expert aid arrives.

6. Choking

a) Mothers always face this problem when their children are small. Remain calm and do not panic. It could aggravate the situation.

b) Make the child lie on his stomach and hit on the back in order to bring out the object.

c) If you find it impossible to retrieve the object, call for medical aid.

7. Animal Bites

a) If the animal is a pet, wash the wound and get yourself injected against tetanus.

b) If the animal is a stray, like dog, cat or a monkey, wash the wound thoroughly under running water for 3-4 minutes. Apply antiseptic soap, like dettol and wash it clean.

c) Get yourself vaccinated against rabies without any delay.

8. Snake Bite

a) Tie a tight cord a little above the bite to restrict the flow of the venom.
b) But, after every half-an hour, remove the cord for a minute before re-tying it to allow the free flow of blood.
c) Get the victim an anti-venom injection without delay.

Some handy tips to be observed when a disease strikes a person or someone is under the bout of fever.

1. Fever

a) Give the victim coffee or tea from time to time. Fruit juices, mixed with glucose, should be given to the patient. Give a liquid diet, like rice gruel, dalia, milk, vegetable soup, to the patient.
b) After the patient recovers, give him a diet of rice and dal, 'khichari', roti and vegetables, devoid of strong spices.

2. Dysentery

a) Give the patient water, mixed with a little salt and sugar, from time to time, to replenish the lost water from the body.
b) Give him a diet of buttermilk, rice gruel, vegetable soup, cooked and mashed bananas, boiled and diluted dals.
c) If the patient is an infant, continue to give mother's milk.

3. Heat Stroke

a) Wrap the victim in water-soaked towel.
b) Put an ice pack on the forehead and the head of the victim.
c) To prevent nausea, give him lemon juice or 'panna' prepared from raw mangoes.
d) In case of fever, consult a doctor.
e) During summers, consume 8-10 glasses of water daily and to prevent heat strokes, drink a glass of pudina (mint) juice before going outdoors.

SUGAR
SALT
WATER

Household

For a homemaker, there can be no place, which is more important than her home. Firstly, there is the all-important part of making a house as per the personal and individual requirements. Then comes the question of doing up the interiors according to one's taste and functional requirements.

Maintaining her home in a neat, clean, comfortable and practical manner is the utmost desire of every woman. In this task she is often deluged with problems of different kinds. There are many facets of the household, which require expert advice. How should the cane furniture be cleaned or how should the garden pests be eliminated? She faces dilemma about the maintenance of her woollens or the ugly stains that dot her expensive apparel. This section deals with solutions to all her problems concerning the household.

SETTING UP THE HOUSE

Owning a house is everyone's ultimate dream. Not many of us are lucky to be able to afford a house and have to settle for a rented one. At best, we settle for a readymade apartment but at the back of our minds is the desire for a house made to order, to suit our individual taste and needs.

Lately, *Vaastu Shastra*, an ancient Indian science of building and architecture, has generated a lot of interest. Houses are being constructed, keeping the rules of '*vaastu*', in mind. '*Vaastu shastra*' directs that the east and north-facing properties are auspicious. It divides the directions into sub-divisions and guides the placement of all rooms according to the specific characteristics of that direction. The basic thumb rules and guidelines are as follows—

♦ The living room should be situated in the central part of the house and should not be in the northern side.

♦ The bedroom slope should be towards the east, which is supposed to bring wealth and prosperity.

♦ The study room should face the east or northeast. All study tables should also face the same direction.

♦ The head of the family should stay in the southwest direction.

♦ Bedrooms can be placed towards the south and your head must be towards the south. One must not sleep with his head pointed towards the north.

♦ The kitchen should be located towards the southeast and the person who cooks should be facing east while cooking.

♦ Northeast direction is considered very sacred and so the *Pooja* room should face this direction.

♦ The dining room should be towards the west.

♦ The bathroom must not face towards the northeast direction.

♦ Avoid using heavy furniture towards the northeast side and keep it the lightest area of the house.

♦ The central axis of the house, which is known as *'dharmas'*, should be kept the lightest and no heavy objects should be stored there.

♦ All valuables should be stored in cupboards, which are placed in the north. Avoid opening the cupboards towards the south.

DESIGNING THE INTERIORS OF YOUR HOUSE

Creating a home is all about aesthetics. A home should be comfortable and functional without looking like a glossy, showroom picture. It should be a place where the family can be at ease and not bother about disturbing the folds of the tablecloth or the arrangements of the cushions. A lived-in look should be incorporated with the elegance of interior designing. There should be no feeling of an antiseptic and surgical cleanliness and coldness. The colour, size, placement of each element has to be thought and requires visualisation. It would help if you begin by drawing out each room along with its dimensions, on a paper. And then begin filling up the spaces. Let us begin by examining each room.

The Living Room

The living room could be a separate space or one, which is combined with the dining area. This is one place, which needs to be kept in order since this is the main area of entertaining friends and visitors. One needs to keep in mind the availability of time, while designing the rooms. Most working couple prefers a simple layout, without too much clutter.

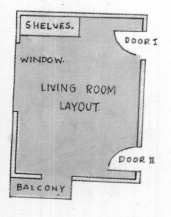

◆ If you are a working couple, you will not be requiring a lot of knick-knacks and decorative items because that will increase your workload and create problems of maintenance. Whereas a lady who stays at home can afford to find time for the cleaning up.

◆ If your area is small, avoid heavy and carved furniture. Light and easily maintainable furniture is the best. Whereas, larger rooms give more scope of maneuvering. Do not go in for heavy carpets if you suffer from asthma or any related problems.

◆ If you have young children or own pets, minimise breakable items. Create space for your music systems and other gadgets.

◆ Use soft and pastel colours on the walls. Build the colour scheme of the soft furnishings accordingly. Keeping the dust factors in mind.

◆ Flooring should be done, keeping the budget; maintenance and the dust factor in mind. Rugs and carpets should be co-ordinated with the colour scheme.

◆ Choose the curtains with a neutral colour so that they can match the upholstery and the carpets.

◆ Give special emphasis on lighting. Lamps, wall brackets and floor lighting should be chosen with care so that they focus on the art works, paintings etc. Soft background light which creates a soft glow in the room, is preferable to bright lighting.

Dining Room

Depending on the room size and numbers, you may, either, want to create a separate room for dining or combine it with the living room. The following factors have to be kept in mind while doing up the dining area.

◆ It should cater for the family as well as a couple of guests. Keep in mind the lifestyle that you follow. If you are one of those who entertain a lot, you need to do up the area in a formal tone whereas the couples who do not entertain much can keep the informal tone in the dining area.

◆ Keep in mind the cabinet space for storage of cutlery, crockery and crystals while ordering for the furniture. A dining table should not be very bulky or huge.

◆ Lighting should be adequate; a central lamp, which focuses on the table, should be catered for.

- While a rectangular dining table offers more space for the dishes, a round one can seat more people.

- Don't go in for carpets in the dining room, instead, settle for a small rug or a colourful *'durry'*. It could be placed under the dining table.

- A nice painting could promote appetite and help in keeping the atmosphere joyous.

- Soft furnishing like mats, napkins, upholstery, drapes and crockery can be coordinated, for a beautiful effect.

- A few indoor plants make the eating experience a pleasant one.

- Try and put in a fresh flower arrangement for a beautiful effect.

Kitchen

This is a very important room and a woman's domain. Never make compromises on the kitchen because it is one place where you will land up spending a lot of time. A kitchen should be large enough for at least two people to work in.

- Start by making a floor plan and drawing a layout. It should be scientifically designed so that the required movements can flow easily.

- The floor should be made of a non-slippery and hard material like marble, cement, or stone.

- The flooring could be vinyl or plain.

- A storeroom and adequate storing space is essential for a kitchen. Cabinets should be designed for easy cleaning and maintenance.

- The power points should be away from the washing area and the cooking area should be away from the electric area. There should be enough power points for gadgets like oven, mixie, toaster etc.

- Coloured or printed tiles help in keeping the walls clean and beautiful.

- The platform should be L-shaped and placed at a convenient height to suit the person who will do the cooking.

- Good ventilation, an exhaust fan and adequate lighting are a necessity.

Bedrooms

- Bedrooms are the place where one spends most of his leisure hours. It should be specially designed to provide the comfort and be Practical.It should essentially contain a double bed, a dressing table and cupboards.

- The bed should be high enough to allow easy cleaning below it. There should be a headrest with adequate space to hold books, and a few decorative items.

- Ventilation should be good and the lighting adequate.

- The walls should neither be bare nor loaded with decorations and paintings. Avoid cluttering of the bedroom.

- The television should find a place in the bedroom along with a music system.

- The lighting should be soft, and romantic. Bedside lamps should be provided for reading.

- The wall unit should contain adequate storage space for clothes etc.

- While wall-to-wall carpets can look very classy, they require a lot of maintenance. Try to fit in some lightweight carpets or rugs for a cosy effect.

- The curtains should be pastel coloured or have light floral motifs.

Bathrooms

Bathrooms have to be well planned for easy cleaning and practicality. While a large family may require at least two such units, a small family may make do with only one.

◆ This room can be done up according to your budget. Right from a shower unit to sunken baths, sky is the limit for the fixtures.

◆ A perfect drainage and plumbing system is a must for the bathrooms. Functionality is the prime consideration.

◆ The flooring should be a non-slip material and the walls should be tiled.

◆ Storage space for soaps, and toiletries should be catered for.

◆ There should be ample lighting to avoid a dingy look.

◆ Ideally the WC should be placed so that it does not face the entrance.

◆ The shower area should be well lit up and adequate ventilation along with an exhaust fan should be planned for.

LIGHTING TIPS

Once the rooms have been planned, you must plan for good lighting for them. To achieve a warm and welcoming effect, ensuring a good lighting system is a must. The mood and use of each room is different and so must the lighting be. The lighting of any particular space must reflect the function of that room. Lights not only provide illumination but they also affect the mood. Sharp lights indicate a formal mood and soft lights are used to set an informal or romantic mood.

Living Room

This is the room where you usually do all the entertaining and you would like to give it the right ambience.

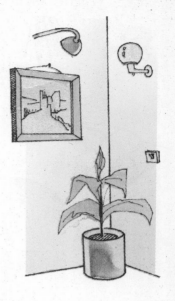

◆ Begin with general lights like the wall, ceiling and table lamps. This should be yellow light.

◆ Choose a focal point, such as a painting or a flower arrangement and highlight this space with a white, halogen light. It is the contrast between the yellow general light and the white light, which draws the attention to the object, which is meant to be highlighted.

◆ The levels of lighting can also make a marked difference, so use your imagination in placing the lights at different level. Shadows thrown up in interesting patterns can also give a very beautiful effect.

◆ A new trend has come up in the scene of lighting the living room and that is the pedestal uplighter, which has a long shaft and cup, rested on it. It throws light upwards, flushing the ceiling. Corner lights should be used to highlight an object.

◆ Picture lights are used to give a dramatic effect to the wall paintings but one can use halogen spots. These are embedded in the ceiling and their focus can be changed to suit the picture spot.

◆ You could also play up certain areas more than the others by using diffused lights and brighter ones, alternatively.

◆ If the dining area is included in the living room, use a chandelier or a hanging light to provide a well-lit and vibrant mood.

Kitchen

◆ The kitchen platform requires good lighting.

◆ Ideally, the light should be a white light and should be placed over the kitchen platform, hidden behind pelmets. It should be concealed but bright.

Bedrooms

◆ Aim to create a calm and peaceful effect by using soft and subtle lighting with minimum glare.

◆ The master bedroom should have low lights, two wall lights and at least two reading lights close to the bed. A picture light should be used if there is a painting on the wall.

◆ The dressing table light should be directly overhead, complimented with one at a lower height.

◆ The reading lamps should be of a higher wattage with a light shade over them.

◆ Avoid ceiling pendants or down lights over the bed.

Bathrooms

◆ The lighting should be flexible enough to provide a soft glow for a relaxing bath in the tub yet strong enough for a shave or a make-up.

◆ The mirror should be well lit up by a light over it. Avoid shadows and maximise the light source so as to light up the face.

◆ Put one light on either side of the mirror for a good effect.

Some More Lighting Tips

◆ Divide the lights of a room, into two types - one for accent and the other for ambience.

◆ Provide for dimmers on all circuits. This can be used to give a dramatic effect. For example, if you are throwing a dinner and the drawing room is lit up with soft lights they can be dimmed out and a chandelier can be put on over the dining area, just as the dinner is being served.

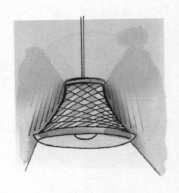

◆ Try to use a layered effect of lighting by combining table lamps, ceiling lights, overhanging lights, wall lights and uplighters.

◆ While planning the lights, take the décor into consideration. Stark and bright lights when used in combination with bright curtains and upholstery can ruin the effect.

◆ Using shadow play with imagination can create a very dramatic and romantic effect. Cane lampshades or cutout leather lampshades throw up interesting shadows on the walls and the floor.

◆ All art objects and pictures should be highlighted.

◆ Walls should be flushed in diffused light.

◆ Dining room should be brightly lit and project a cheerful ambience.

◆ Avoid halogens in the children's room as they emit heat. Use tubelights wherever possible because they reduce your electricity costs.

◆ Overhead lights in the drawing room are not very classy. Use concealed and soft lights to give a soothing effect.

◆ A corner of the room can be lit up with a floor lamp. Concealed lights should be used in rooms with false ceilings to give it a larger look.

COLOUR TIPS

Colours play a very important role in designing the interiors of a home. One can create the right ambience and mood by playing imaginatively with colours. Each room requires a different colour scheme to bring out the relevant ambience. Knowledge of the colour wheel is essential to work out a good colour scheme.

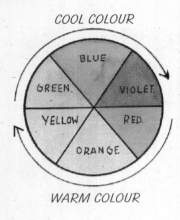

COOL COLOUR

BLUE
GREEN   VIOLET
YELLOW   RED.
ORANGE

WARM COLOUR

◆ The colour wheel can be divided into two parts - the cool colours are blue, green, and violet while the warm colours are red, yellow and orange.

◆ Cool colours create a restful and soothing atmosphere while the warm colours cheer up a room that is cold and windy.

◆ The two main schemes to work on are - the monochromatic scheme in which one takes only one colour but utilises different shades of the colour, together·with some neutral colours to form a restful colour scheme.

◆ The related colour scheme is the one where one combines shades that are side by side on the colour wheel, for a refreshing effect.

◆ Pastel colours create the illusion of space. A small area painted in a light shade will appear larger than if it were painted in dark colours.

◆ Dark colours absorb heat and light colours reflect it.

◆ Use a dark colour to cut out the glare in a very bright room; paint a dark room white, to get maximum light and make it look bright.

◆ Colour changes under different light conditions. For instance, a dark colour looks brighter in a large, well-lit room.

◆ Pale colours tend to look insipid under artificial light and blues as well as greens change shade under fluorescent light.

◆ Colour is affected by the colour next to it.

◆ Yellow appears cool when it is placed against a dark brown background but it will appear warmer when placed against green.

◆ A white lamp blends into a beige background but will stand out with dramatic effect against a dark backdrop.

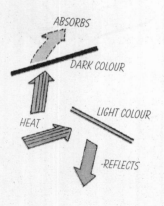

ABSORBS

DARK COLOUR

LIGHT COLOUR

HEAT

-REFLECTS

TIPS ON AVOIDING CLUTTER

Finding a thing in a cluttered household requires a lot of time, effort and patience. It makes the house look untidy and gives a wrong impression to people who come to visit you. Getting organised saves a lot of time as well as effort. The unnecessary items that accumulate over the years, end up in taking up precious space.

◆ Clutter can be expensive and takes up valuable space. Maybe your garage is so full of useless stuff that your car is standing outside the garage and getting rusted.

◆ Don't make excuses to clear up unwanted things and don't defer the action. You may feel that you will require those things like screws, unused utensils, old shoes, clothes, electric wires, and unidentifiable spares, some day. Generally speaking, anything you have not used for two years will never be required again. So throw them or give them away.

◆ Go by the logic—use it or throw it or give away.

◆ Find the best place for everything. Keep things like keys, scissors, sewing kit, tool box, torch, emergency lights etc, in fixed place. This will save you from hunting for them and reduce the clutter, too.

◆ Whatever doesn't work, throw away. Don't wait for one day when you will find the time to repair it. Most probably, you will never find the time.

◆ Have a proper filing system for things like letters, photographs, information brochures, stationery, guarantee cards for the gadgets, postage, recipes, catalogues etc.

◆ Spend at least one day every six months, clearing all the junk like useless gadgets, papers and scraps.

◆ Get money out of the junk by selling it instead of hoarding it.

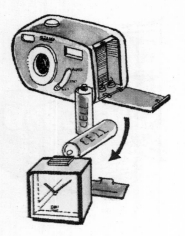

♦ Recycle things immediately. A battery cell, which cannot function in your camera, might still work in the quartz clock.

♦ Things like little scraps of leftover cloth, wool or greeting cards can be made to good use and promote creativity in the children. Give them such tasks during the holidays.

CLEANING & SHINING

Years back, when I bought my first carpet, I did not know how to clean it or maintain it. Since it was a very expensive Kashmiri carpet, gifted to me by my mother, I wanted to be absolutely sure about its upkeep. It took me a long time to learn all about the cleaning and maintenance of carpets. Sometimes, even small things like shining the brassware or cleaning the leather articles can become a source of anxiety if one does not have the knowledge to deal with the subject. Since, some of the household articles are expensive and quite often it is not possible to discard them, one needs to know the ways and means of elongating their life span. Given here are some valuable tips on handling the subject.

♦ Your old shoes will shine like new if you apply a tea decoction before the shoe polish.

♦ Sticky marks left behind after peeling off labels can be removed by applying white spirit.

♦ If leather shoes get wet, especially during the monsoon, drain off the water and stuff them with newspaper. This will speed up the drying process and the shoes will retain their original shape.

♦ While mopping the floor, add 2 teaspoons of salt to the water to keep flies at bay.

TEA

- Rub faded carpets or mats with warm water and turpentine. This will bring back the original colour and shine.

- Clean your window glass with some chalk powder. Then take a piece of cloth and rub well. The glass will begin to shine.

- To clean dirty and greasy kitchen napkins, boil them with a little detergent and washing soda. Remove from heat and add some paraffin. Boil for another 30 minutes.

- Sprinkle a little boric acid powder on bathroom tiles before washing, for economical and sparkling results.

- To remove hot water marks from polished tables, make a thin paste of salad oil and salt. Apply a little on the marks and allow standing for an hour. Rub well with a soft duster.

- To keep a vacuum flask clean and odour free, fill up half the flask with vinegar, hot water and pieces of egg shell.

- Old leather bags can be polished with shoe polish to make them shine.

- Old leather shoes, bags, belts etc. can be given a new lease of life with a single coat of fabric paint. They can also be polished with a clear liquid polish.

- After washing, stick wet hankies on the clean tiles of sidewalls of the bathroom. They will not fall down when dry and will look well ironed when removed.

- Dab some aftershave lotion on your shoes and rub them lightly. They will get a super shine.

- To clean porcelain vases, scrub them with a brush dipped in salted water.

- To get sparkling clean toilets, use a few drops of fabric whitener.

- For a sparkling mirror, squirt a little toothpaste on a damp newspaper and scrub it.

- While swabbing floor, add 1 tablespoon of detergent powder to the water. This will clean the floor while keeping the mop clean.

- Slip one or two old socks at the end of a rod to make an effective cobweb remover.

- To renew lost shine in an old painting, rub it with a slice of bread. Then, using upward strokes, clean with slices of raw potatoes.

- Place a thick aluminium foil under your ironing sheet. You will be able to do your ironing very neatly and swiftly.

- Sprinkle lots of salt over a dirty carpet and let it be on for a minute or two. When you rub the salt vigorously, the dirt will also come out along with the salt.

- To clean bathroom plastic ware, apply some kerosene and detergent powder on them. Keep aside for about 5 minutes and rub with a nylon scrubber. Wash well with lukewarm water for the sparkling look.

- Clean marble flooring with a mixture of hydrogen peroxide and water mixed in ratio of 1:4.

- To clean mattresses and quilts, coat with starch solution and dry in strong sunlight. Once dry, brush the starch off. All marks and spots will disappear with the starch.

- To clean glass articles, soak them in a mixture of vinegar and water, overnight. Rinse with a mild cleaning liquid.

- To remove rust spots from metal, rub gently with an ink erasir.

- A mixture of liquid ammonia and detergent powder is excellent for cleaning cabinets, refrigerators and garbage pails.

- To clean a candle stand made of any material, especially glass, and place it in the deep freezer for an hour. The wax will chip off easily.

◆ Wipe your window grills with a cloth dipped in kerosene to keep away cobwebs.

◆ To protect the window panes from paint spots, wash the glass with soap and wipe off the soap with a damp cloth after the painting is over.

◆ To clean the shoes of your kid, take a little coconut oil and a swab of cotton, rub it into the shoes. They will shine like brand new.

◆ Old leather bags and belts can be made to look new by rubbing with cotton wool soaked in a solution of ½ teaspoon rose water, 1 teaspoon glycerine and ½ teaspoon coconut oil.

◆ To remove grease marks from wallpaper, place a blotting paper over them and press with a hot iron.

◆ Banana peels can be an excellent substitute for the shoe polish. Rub a leather shoe with a fresh banana peel and then polish with a soft cloth.

◆ To make your old shoes shine like new, polish them with a tea decoction before using a normal shoe polish.

◆ Polish mirrors and glassware with a black tea decoction.

◆ To clear dust and grease from exhaust fans and bulbs in the kitchen, wipe with coconut fibre dipped in kerosene. Follow this by a good scrub with a cotton cloth dipped in washing powder.

◆ Use a typewriter eraser to remove the dirt collected between the floor and the wall tiles of your rooms.

◆ To get a special shine, hold the polishing brush before a heater or a lamp to warm it. Now polish the shoes with the brush to give them the sheen.

◆ Window panes, aluminium sheets, wash basin mirrors, tiles and commodes will remain sparkling clean if rubbed over with a piece of lemon and wiped dry with a cheese cloth.

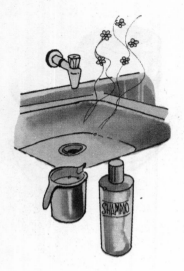

♦ To bring back the gloss in ivory products which have got tarnished due to humid weather, rub them with lemon slices.

♦ Wash the washbasin with diluted shampoo for a lingering fragrance.

♦ To clean dirt from the crevices of bathroom tiles, scrub with a mixture of a tablespoon each of lemon juice, detergent and phenyl.

♦ Use Brasso to remove stains from glass, sunmica, the fridge or marble. It can be used to clean almost anything. Apply Brasso with a cotton swab, for best results.

♦ You can polish your silverware with a paste of gramflour and ½ a lemon for a sparkling result.

♦ If oil has leaked from the car on the garage floor, just spread out a damp newspaper over the oil stains. Leave it in place till the newspaper is dry. When you remove the paper, the stains will be gone.

♦ To shine brass articles, rub them with a mixture of 2 teaspoons of vinegar and $1^1/_2$ teaspoon cleaning powder. Wash in running water, dry them with a napkin and watch them sparkle.

♦ Remove pet hair from upholstery and cushions by rubbing a damp sponge over the required area.

♦ To clean artificial flowers, shake them in a bag containing a cup of salt.

CLEANING POWDER   VINEGER

CLOTHES

Clothes are subject of interest for any homemaker, especially if she happens to be a woman. They are an indispensable item on her agenda. The upkeep, maintenance and cleaning of expensive sarees or apparel can be quite a daunting task. Here are some tried and tested tips to help you in your endeavour.

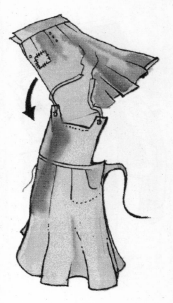

◆ Old and unused *'dupattas'* can be used as lining material for dresses.

◆ Old skirts can be opened at the seams and used to make aprons.

◆ When the collar becomes frayed, detach it from the shirt and stitch it back again on the reverse side. The collar will look as good as new.

◆ If you want to prevent your favourite jeans from fading, soak them in cold water before washing them.

◆ To starch silk saris, use a few drops of gum in half a bucket of water.

◆ To retain the crispness of silk saris or dresses, add a little gram flour to the water in the last rinse.

◆ For sharp creases on trousers, rub a candle on the reverse, before ironing them.

◆ To make your white clothes sparkle, add a tablespoon of kerosene when you soak them in water and rinse as usual.

◆ After washing silk garments, add a little limejuice to a bucket of water and rinse them in this solution. The silk will shine.

◆ To remove grime from shirt cuffs and collars, rub talcum powder liberally till it forms a thick coating. Leave overnight. Wash the next day.

LIME

SILK CLOTH

◆ Pressure cook about 300 gm *'moong dal'* and mash it thoroughly when cold. To this add a bucketful of water and strain through a sieve to remove the residue of cooked *'dal'*. Soak your silk saris in this water for 5 minutes and rinse in water 2-3 times. Dry in the shade and iron them. The sari will be soft and the *'zari'* will look brighter. There is no need to use any detergent. This quantity of *'dal'* water is sufficient for 2-3 saris.

◆ For shiny finish to silk saris, dissolve one packet (10 gms) of gelatine in 1 cup of boiling water. Add this to ¼ bucket warm water. Dip the washed silk saris in this solution and dry in the shade.

◆ If you wash silk saris at home, add the juice of a lime to the cleaning liquid. The juice prevents the saris from getting discoloured and also keeps the silk soft.

◆ To starch silk suits at home, use liquid gum mixed in water. When the suits are dry, iron them.

◆ If you turn the cuffs and collars inside out before putting them in the washing machine, they will come out cleaner.

◆ If washing delicate or lace-edged articles, put them into a pillowcase before placing them in the washing machine.

◆ To make new tights last longer, wash and rinse them. Squeeze them out gently. Secure them in a plastic bag and freeze them overnight. Thaw them out and hang to dry.

◆ Never iron knitted garments. When they are taken off the line, fold them in half, easing them into shape. The clothes will keep their shape and last much longer.

◆ To remove sticky labels on new clothes, turn them inside out and run a hot iron on them.

◆ To rid clothes of odours, add a few drops of liquid ammonia to the water while washing.

ASPIRINS

◆ To remove the odour of perspiration from clothes, dip them in a bucket of water containing 3 aspirins.

◆ Dry-clean your *sarees* at home by soaking them in water to which 3-teaspoon acetic acid and surf have been added. Squeeze the water out and resoak them in water containing 3 teaspoons of acetic acid and starch. Rinse; dry with a Turkish towel and iron while they are still damp.

◆ Adding a little salt to the starch while starching clothes will prevent them from sticking together.

◆ Always soak the *saree* fall in salted water for a few hours before stitching it on the *sarees*. This will prevent the bleeding of the colour at a later date.

◆ Ironing clothes on an aluminium sheet helps maintain the sharp creases of the garments.

◆ To clean dirty collars, use shampoo on them.

◆ Place some camphor or cloves between your woollens to keep them free from germs.

◆ To remove chewing gum from your clothes, place the garments in a plastic bag and freeze it. You can then flick off the hardened gum easily. Alternatively, soak the garment in white vinegar and wash off. Or rub the area with the white of an egg before washing it off.

◆ Chewing gum can also be removed from clothing by scraping off and then using white spirit for the residue.

◆ Delicate fabrics like georgette can be washed with bath soap as a detergent may spoil their colour.

◆ Add a pinch of salt to the water before adding the blue powder. The clothes will not come out with blue patches, if you do so.

◆ Coloured cotton outfits tend to have white patches on them after they are starched. To avoid such patches, add a few drops of liquid blue to the starch solution before dipping the clothes in it.

◆ To prevent colours of different garments from running onto each other, add 1 tablespoon of vinegar to ½ a bucket of water, while soaking the clothes.

WOOLLENS

I still remember that beautiful 'Pashmina' shawl presented to me on my wedding day, by my mother-in-law. It was ruined because I did not know the art of preserving it. I shed many a tear over the moth eaten shawl. I was young and inexperienced at that time. It took me years to learn all the tricks about storing the precious woollens I owned. Then

VINEGAR

GLYCERINE

I decided to share my secret tips with the other inexperienced, young women, who could face the same dilemma as I did.

Washing and Storing

◆ Always wash woollen garments in lukewarm water. Never in hot or cold water.

◆ Crush and soak '*reetha*' seeds, overnight. Make a frothy solution by rubbing the pieces with hand in the morning. Soak the woollens in this solution and rub gently. If the coloured garments bleed, add a teaspoon of salt or alum to the solution. This will also prevent the woollen garments from shrinking. Don't soak the coloured garments for long. Rinse well.

◆ Add a teaspoon of glycerine to the water in which woollens are washed. This prevents them from shrinking and losing their texture

◆ To the last rinse, add 2 drops of ammonia or glycerine. Keep the garment soaked in the solution for about 2 minutes. The garment will shine like new.

◆ Never hang woollens on the clothesline or dry them in direct sunlight. Squeeze out the water gently and wrap them in a dry towel to remove excess moisture. Dry them on a flat surface on which a clean, dried towel has been spread.

◆ To remove wrinkles, cover the garment with damp cloth and iron lightly.

DAMPED CLOTH

◆ Before sending woollen garments for dry cleaning, it is better to remove the extra dirt from the collars, cuffs and pockets. To do so, spread the garment on a flat surface, which has been lined with blotting paper. Now soak a piece of clean cloth in petrol and rub on the dirt. The dirt will leave the garment and appear on the blotting paper.

◆ Never pack woollens immediately after sunning them. Put naphthalene balls in between the folds. Line the steel box with a sheet of newspaper or a clean cloth. An old bedcover will also serve the purpose. Layer the bottom with dried *neem, tulsi* (basil) or tobacco leaves. Heavier woollens should always be stored at the bottom and the lighter ones on the top so that one can take out the lighter woollens easily at the beginning of the winter season.

NEPHTHLENE BALLS

◆ Instead of using naphthalene balls while storing woollen garments, put layers of *neem* leaves between the garments.

◆ To preserve woollens, place some camphor tablets and cloves between the folds.

◆ Oil stains on woollen clothes will fade if rubbed with a mixture of curd and salt. Leave the mixture on for about 10 minutes and rinse with cold water.

◆ Woollens kept away for a long time should be steamed for 5-10 minutes before use. This removes the odour and softens the fabric.

SEWING TIPS

◆ If you are fed up with the problem of the sewing thread knotting up, break off the thread from the reel and put a knot with the broken end.

◆ If you have problems while threading a needle, use a contrast background. For a dark colour thread, use a white paper for background and for a white colour thread; use a dark paper for the background.

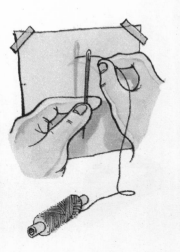

◆ To sharpen a sewing machine needle, stitch through a sandpaper.

◆ To cut off buttons from a garment without damaging it, slip a comb under the buttons and cut them off with a blade.

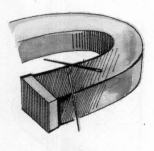

- A tailor had once advised me not to use too long a thread while hemming. A long thread will get knotted easily. The hemming may also come off in a short time. Use short lengths of thread.

- Keep a small magnet in your sewing kit. This will help you in finding the lost needles and holding them together.

- To sew buttons with four holes, use one length of thread for one side and another length for the other side. This will prevent the button coming off if one of the threads breaks.

- To stitch a button in the garment, place it in the spot and stick with some cellotape. This will help you in fixing it easily.

- To make your own machine oil, take 2 drops of mustard oil, 2 drops of coconut oil, 2 drops of kerosene and ½ a drop of petrol.

- To stitch a thick fabric easily, rub a little wax at the spot of stitching. The needle will pierce the fabric easily.

- For a neat buttonhole, apply a little colourless nail varnish at the spot, on the fabric. This will stiffen the fabric and making a gash will become easy. Thereafter, the buttonhole can be made easily.

ODOUR REMOVAL TIPS

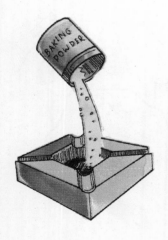

The treacherous monsoon months with their humid and stale odour, and the stale smell of the fungus-ridden air, can be a real nuisance to the olfactory glands. No woman would like her home to smell anything but fragrant. With a little effort and a little help stunning results can be achieved.

- Jasmine or any fragrant fresh flowers act as excellent air fresheners without any hazardous effects on the environment.

◆ To remove the odour of garlic or fish from your hands, wash them with limejuice or salted water, before applying soap.

◆ To get rid of the smell of kerosene from the hands, wash them with gramflour.

◆ To get rid of stale cigarette smell from an ashtray, sprinkle ¼ teaspoon of baking powder in it.

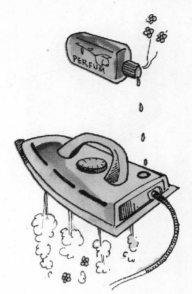

◆ Cigarette odour can be eliminated, from a room, by lighting a candle.

◆ Soak a piece of cotton in phenyl and place it in the bathroom. The fresh smell lingers for days together.

◆ Squeezed out lemon halves will absorb food odours from the fridge.

◆ Add a few drops of cologne to a large, shallow pan filled with water and freeze. Keep this scented ice under the fan in your room. It feels good during the hot season.

◆ To remove a strong odour from a used bottle, rinse it with clean water and then drop a lighted matchstick inside and close the lid. Open the lid after 2 minutes and rinse again with clean water.

◆ For lingering fragrance, add a few drops of perfume to the water in your steam iron.

◆ The odour from the toilet can be eliminated instantly if you light a matchstick in the toilet.

◆ For a lingering and lasting fragrance in your clothes, place used bottles of perfume in your cupboard.

FURNITURE

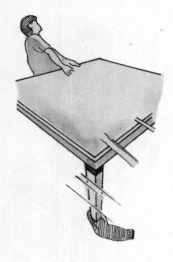

Buying good furniture can be an expensive thing in these days of inflation. It is rare to come across solid wooden furniture, which will stand the test of time. Gone are the days when teak wood furniture, handed from generation to generation, decorated the house. If you are fortunate enough to own a good piece, you must take adequate care of it and if you don't own one, it is still important to know how to make a bad piece of furniture last for a long time.

◆ Slip old socks over the furniture legs while moving them to prevent the floor from getting scratched.

◆ Scratches on furniture will disappear if you apply cod liver oil and leave it on for 24 hours before polishing.

◆ Clean your bamboo or cane furniture with salt water for an extra shine.

◆ Applying brown shoe polish to wooden furniture and polishing with a dry cloth lends an excellent sheen to it.

◆ To clean a wooden table covered with white stains, rub it with a paste of cigarette ash and olive oil.

◆ To make wooden furniture shine again, take 2 teaspoon of used tea leaves, dry them in the sun. Put them in a muslin cloth and add 8 drops of mustard oil. Tie it in a bundle and rub it on the furniture. They will gleam like new.

◆ Cleaning the wooden furniture with a mixture or mustard oil and kerosene will bring a shine to it.

◆ Make your own furniture polish by adding 2 tablespoon olive oil and 1 tablespoon vinegar to 750 ml of hot water. Stir will and use it while it is hot. Dust the furniture to remove all dirt and then rub the surface with a rag dipped in the polish.

◆ Add 1 tablespoon of turpentine oil in 750 ml water in which detergent powder has been added. Wipe the

furniture with this solution to bring sheen to the furniture.

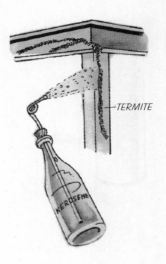

TERMITE

◆ Termites are the biggest enemies of wood and eliminating them is a tedious task. Termites can be removed from wooden furniture by spraying with kerosene oil.

◆ Polishing the cane furniture with kerosene make it last longer and retains its shine, too.

◆ To clean enamel painted wooden furniture, wipe them with a solution of lukewarm water with washing powder.

◆ Add a little coconut oil to a mug full of water and clean dusty wooden furniture with a little cotton wool dipped in this solution.

◆ To get rid of white ants from the wooden shelves, pour a mixture of camphor powder and liquid paraffin in strategic locations.

◆ To remove candle wax from wooden surfaces, soften the wax with a hairdryer and then wipe off.

◆ If your wrought iron furniture gets spots of rust, wipe with kerosene oil and apply some grease so that the rust will not spread. This type of furniture can be cleaned with hot water in which a little ammonia has been added.

◆ To clean leather furniture, use sandalwood soap. For a good shine to the leather rub with the white of an egg. The stain spots of these furniture pieces can be removed with petrol. If the leather is drying up, apply some castrol oil and the suppleness will remain intact.

◆ For upholstered furniture, use a vacuum cleaner every week.

◆ Plastic and moulded furniture can be cleaned with warm water to which a little detergent has been added. Later clean with some cold water. One must keep this type of furniture away from direct sunlight otherwise they can get discoloured.

PESTS

'Pests'- the very name explains their nature. They can be a great nuisance, whether it is the rat, cockroach, and ant or fly; it is difficult to live with the lot. Destruction is their second name. If you want your home to remain safe and free from pests, try the solutions given in this section.

◆ Make a paste of DDT or Gamaxine powder with a little water and seal ant holes with it. The ants will vanish in a jiffy.

◆ Environment friendly pesticide can be made by grinding together 4 onions, 4 red chillies, 2 garlic flakes, keeping it for a day and then mixing with 4 litres of water. Spray this around the house to get rid of pests, especially cockroaches.

◆ Neem leaves are an excellent remedy for most pests. Burning a mixture of incense and dry neem leaves will keep the mosquitoes away.

◆ Hairspray is an excellent insecticide.

◆ Mix a cup of gram flour with a teaspoon each of boric powder and fine sugar. Knead and divide the dough into 30 small balls and dry them in the sun. Place the balls around the house to keep cockroaches at bay. Repeat the process every two months.

◆ Dip *'agarbattis'* in baygon or kerosene and then light them. The fumes will repel mosquitoes and flies.

◆ To get rid of flies, spread some jam and Baygon crystals on a slice of bread and place it in a saucer. The flies will get attracted to it and die.

◆ To keep insects at bay, pour a small quantity of scented phenyl in plastic containers and keep them on the windowsill.

◆ Place tobacco leaves under the carpets for an effective pesticide. Tobacco leaves can also be used to keep insects away from woollens.

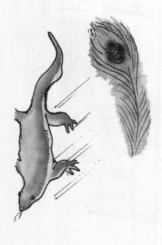

◆ Perch a peacock feather somewhere in the room to ward off lizards. Raw egg shells is another thing that lizards detest, so place a few of them wherever, you feel, the lizards reside.

◆ While mopping the floor, add a few drops of 'mehendi' oil to ward off mosquitoes.

◆ Place a ball of cotton soaked in peppermint oil near a rat hole. The rats will flee.

◆ Don't throw away used mosquito mats. Keep them in a corner of the room to drive away ants. Burn them to get rid of mosquitoes.

◆ Keep dried red chillies in your wardrobe to protect your silk and woollen garments from silverfish.

◆ Good old naphthalene balls are still the best remedy, to drive away pests from the drains.

◆ Keep some camphor tied in a piece of muslin cloth in a corner of a room to keep insects away.

◆ Dry *neem* twigs tied in a cloth and placed in cupboards and suitcases work as excellent eco-friendly, insect repellants.

◆ To get rid of ants, draw a line with a chalk around the ant holes and along the walls where they appear.

◆ Place a small piece of camphor in the dustbin to keep stale odour and vermin at bay.

◆ Burn dried orange peel in charcoal or saw dust to drive away mosquitoes and other insects. The smoke also gives a sweet smell.

◆ Dissolve 3 camphor tablets in a cup of water and place it under the bed to keep mosquitoes away.

◆ To get rid of rats and mice, place cotton swabs soaked in turpentine, at strategic locations around the house.

◆ Sprinkle some dry *neem* leaves in bookshelves to keep away the white ants.

CAMPHOR

◆ To get rid of mosquitoes, keep a used mosquito mat on top of a gas lantern.

◆ A garlic flake dipped in castor oil and placed in a mosquito coil will make the mosquitoes disappear.

◆ Dry lemon peels in the sun and use them as insect repellents in cupboards etc.

◆ Spread peppercorns under mattresses to avoid insects and bed bugs.

◆ A blue night bulb will keep the mosquitoes away from the bedroom.

◆ Mix one tablespoon of gemaxin powder with one tablespoon of kerosene oil and make into a paste. Apply the paste to all corners and along the wall, with a brush. The ants will vanish in seconds.

◆ Cucumber peels are excellent ant repellants. Next time ants invade your household, keep bits of cucumber skins wherever you think the ants congregate.

◆ To get rid of ants, pour a few drops of kerosene along the ant-trail.

◆ Add ½ teaspoon of asafoetida to ½ a cup of water and pour into all the holes or cracks where white ants exist. After a few days, they will disappear.

◆ Borax powder sprinkled under the paper on the shelves keeps off silver fish.

◆ To keep moths and insects away from upholstered furniture, sprinkle powdered alum or a few cloves down the crevices and under the carpets.

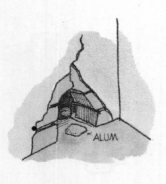

◆ Rats can be eliminated by placing pieces of alum near their holes.

◆ If you clean the floor with a solution of alum and phenyl, the flies will not dare to sit off the floors.

◆ Broken eggshells will keep lizards away from the place.

ECONOMY TIPS

Economy plays a very important role in housekeeping. 'Waste not want not'- is a very apt saying. Little savings can go an amazingly long way. Even the little wastage that seems so inconsequential, can lead to a lot of strain on the family budget. It is very simple to control wastage and practise good economic sense.

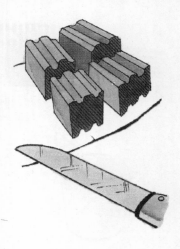

◆ After washing clothes in a machine, use the soap water to clean bathrooms, sinks or toilets.

◆ Clean your flask with hot water to increase its life. It will also remain odour-free.

◆ Candles and soaps will last longer if you place them in the freezer for a couple of hours.

◆ Make your own metal polish at home by mixing 30 gms oxalic acid and 1 tablespoon hydrochloric acid in 600 ml boiling water.

◆ Cut a detergent bar into four pieces before using. It will last longer.

◆ Collect leftover wax from burnt out candles, melt it in a pan with a coloured wax crayon. Put a wick into a mould and pour the molten wax into it. When set, paint attractive designs over the candle to decorate it.

◆ Almost discharged, leakproof cells can be rejuvenated by putting them overnight, in salt solution (7 gms of salt in a litre of water).

SALT (7 GMS)

1 LITRE

CELL

◆ Place a piece of paper between the last cell and the lid of the torch. This will prevent the cells from leaking.

◆ Empty detergent powder sachets and covers can be used as scrubbers for washbasins, tiles and kitchen platform.

◆ Make your own bolster by putting old, soft, discarded garments into an old sari or bed sheet and rolling out like a bolster. Now sew this on both ends and put on an attractive cover.

PARAFFIN

Expensive car polish can be substituted by a bucket of hot water with a cupful of paraffin added to it.

◆ Torn carpets can be cut into smaller rugs and mats. The edges must be secured with blanket stitch in matching wool.

◆ Putting them in an old socks and washing the washbasin with them can use up leftover soap pieces.

◆ Melting the bits and pieces of a candle, kerosene and a dash of turmeric powder in a tin can make wood polish at home. Heat and allow cooling and setting, before using.

◆ Don't throw away piece of attractive waste cloth. Stitch them together, instead, in different shapes and sizes to make bright and beautiful embroidered designs.

◆ Make an old blanket into a comfortable baby sleeping bag. All you need to do is cut the blanket to the right size, hem the edges and sew up the sides. If you want, you could put in a front opening and a zip.

◆ Use your old denims for making denim dungarees or a pinafore dress for your toddler. Denim is ideal for children's clothes because it is so hardwearing.

◆ Old T-shirts can be converted into children's nighties. Just slip some elastic around the neck. If they are faded, you could dye them to make them more colourful.

◆ For homemade bathroom mats, insert foam sheets into old pillow covers or fancy cushion covers and stitch up the edges neatly.

◆ Discarded sleeves from woollen clothes make terrific leg warmers.

◆ Cut out the old Turkish towels into small squares and stitch the sides to be used as body scrubs.

◆ Refrigerated candles for 5-6 hours before use. This will help the candle burn longer and less wax will drip.

◆ It is amazing how the cost of candles keeps going up each year. Here is another tip to make your candle last longer. Candles burn longer if you apply salt on the wick.

◆ Once you have used up toothpaste, don't throw away the tube. Cut it open and you will find enough paste to clean your gold or silver ornaments, sinks, mirrors and even refrigerators, with a toothbrush.

◆ Don't throw away used mosquito repellant mats. Dip the mats in water for ½ a minute and dry it in the open for not more than ½ a minute. It becomes as good as new. Re-use the other side also.

ENERGY SAVING TIPS

Wastage of energy resources is a very serious global concern. With dwindling and shrinking of the natural resources and the burgeoning population, the next century may see world wars over things like petroleum, water and coal, etc. It is the duty of every member of this earth to save the valuable resources and chip in his own bit. Whether it is petrol, cooking gas, electricity, water or paper, we all have to make a combined effort to conserve the available resources.

Most people own vehicles these days. If we all were to make an optimum use of the fuel, we can save a lot of money besides making a valuable contribution towards the noble cause of energy-conservation.

You can improve fuel economy and get more mileage from every drop of fuel by the using the following tips—

◆ Reduce the idling time. Switch off the engine whenever you have to halt for more than one minute. Whether it is at a traffic light or while chatting with a friend, switch off and re-start. Not only do you save fuel, you also help in reducing the pollution.

- When warming up a cold engine, especially during the cold, winter mornings, allow the engine to idle until the temperature gauge pointer comes up to 'C' position. Once it reaches that position, the engine is sufficiently warm to start off.

- Driving at a steady speed as per the requirements of the road condition and traffic, instead of accelerating and braking erratically, saves a lot of fuel. Avoid spurts and bursts of speed, especially in city driving.

- Start off slowly. Fast starts just a little away from traffic lights or the stop signs will consume unnecessary fuel and shorten engine life, too.

- Keep a check on the tyre pressure. Under inflated tyres can waste fuels due to increased running resistance of the tyres. Maintaining a correct tyre pressure will give you more mileage.

- Change gears according to your speed. Drive at the right gear for optimum benefit. It will help in saving your car from unnecessary wear and tear, also.

- Avoid excessive baggage. The heavier the load, the more fuel the vehicle consumes. Remove all unnecessary luggage while driving.

- Keep the air cleaner-clean. Dirty air cleaner causes the carburetion system to supply too much fuel to the engine. And a waste of fuel occurs due to incomplete combustion.

- Keep the spark plugs clean and de-carbonised. Accumulation of carbon delays the starting of the engine. A regular cleaning with emery paper removes most of the carbon deposits.

- Avoid unnecessary halts. Try to maintain a slow and steady movement. Constant slowing down and accelerating guzzles up a lot of fuel.

Saving on Cooking Gas

◆ Cooking on the smaller burner is wiser. There is a lot of wastage of heat when you use the big burner for small vessels.

◆ Use vessels with a wide bottom so that the entire lot of heat and flame is covered and there is no wastage from the sides.

◆ Once the water or the liquids reach the boiling point, reduce the heat and bring it to simmer. Keeping the flame on high will just waste gas.

◆ If you are cooking in a cooker, reduce the flame to 'Sim' as soon as the cooker whistles. Make a note of the time and go by the time instead of going by the number of whistles.

◆ Keep all the ingredients ready; at hand and then light the gas burner. Don't light and then go hunting for the *masalas* or the utensils.

◆ Cover the utensil while the cooking is in progress. This way, you save on gas while retaining the valuable nutrients in your cooking. Open cooking is neither healthy nor wise.

◆ Use a pressure cooker wherever and whenever possible.

◆ Avoid heating and reheating. Plan your mealtime and cooking so that you don't have to keep heating the food. This way, you not only save on the cooking gas but you also conserve the nutrients in your food.

Saving on Electric Energy

Electric energy is another area where one has to be judicious. If you are fed up with the power cuts that hound your everyday life, remember that power saved is power gained. Saving electric energy will help you save money as well as conserve the energy that is in short supply. We often waste a lot of electricity through improper use or negligence.

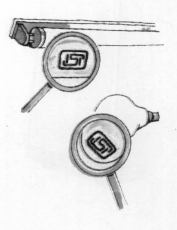

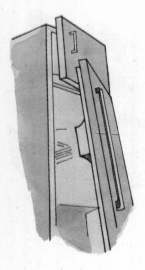

Fridge

◆ A regular defrosting of the fridge can save electricity by increasing the cooling efficiency of the fridge.

◆ Avoid opening the fridge door frequently. Opening the door very often hinders cooling and more electricity is required in running the fridge as the idling time is reduced.

◆ Keep the items in an organised manner so that you are aware of the placing of different items. That way, you do not have to keep the door open and search for each item.

◆ Plan your menu in the morning so that you can take out all the required vegetables for each meal, at one go.

◆ Placing the right thing at the right place will help in the efficient preservation of the food items. Dairy products should be stored according to their perishibility. Butter should be kept in a covered container while non-vegetarian items like meat and fish should be kept in polythene bags and stored in the freezer. Fruits and vegetables should be kept in the crisper and chocolates should be stored in the chiller.

◆ Also check if the lining on the fridge door, which comprises a rubber gasket, is tight enough and there is no leakage of the cold air from within the fridge. The fridge door should shut properly.

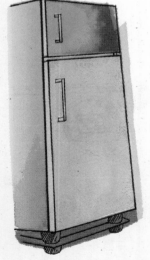

Toaster

◆ Clean the bread crumbs with a clean dry cloth.

◆ Never use the moist cloth.

◆ Don't scratch the inner surface of the toaster to remove stubborn stains.

Mixie/Grinder

◆ Do not put a hot or a very cold substance in the blender.

◆ Crush ice before adding it to the blender.

◆ Increase the speed of the motor from low, medium and then high and do the vice-versa to stop it.

◆ The blender should not be filled above $^3/_4$ its size.

◆ Do not keep the motor on for more than 2 minutes at a time. Give it a rest of 15 secs if you have to do again.

Washing Machine

◆ Never use the washing machine without water.

◆ Water tank should be filled as per indications.

◆ Don't overburden your gadget.

◆ Always use good quality washing powder.

◆ Clean and dry the machine after use.

STAINS

Stains can ruin the best of the clothes, furniture, and upholstery. Although it may seem difficult to remove the stubborn stains, it is not really difficult to do so if one knows the trick. Most stains can be removed if action is taken immediately. Older stains are hard to remove.

◆ To remove stubborn ink stains from clothes, rub the area with a cotton bud soaked in eau-de-cologne.

◆ An easy way to remove henna stains from clothes is to soak the stained portion in hot milk for half an hour. Then rinse in cold water and clean with a brush.

◆ Water stains can be removed from wooden surface by wiping with alcohol.

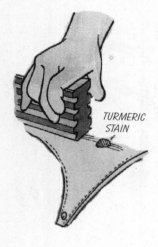

TURMERIC STAIN

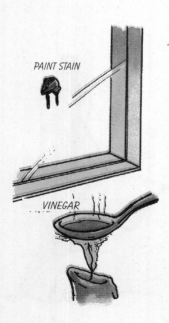

PAINT STAIN

VINEGAR

◆ To remove turmeric stains from clothes, rub a dry detergent bar soap over the stain and leave it for an hour before washing it off.

◆ To remove stubborn stains from porcelain, especially in small crevices, rub a dry mixture of soda bicarb and table salt with just a drop of water into them. The stains will disappear.

◆ To remove '*paan*' stains, cover the stains with curd or limejuice and wash after a couple of hours.

◆ A mixture of vinegar and salt removes stains and stale smells from flower vases.

◆ Remove stubborn coffee or tea stains from your china cups, by scrubbing them with salt, or a paste of baking soda and water, or a 50-50 mixture of salt and white vinegar.

◆ To remove stains from garments apply a little limejuice over the area and wash.

◆ In order to remove tea, coffee or iodine stains; dip the stained area in a solution of hot water and borax. Don't dip the entire cloth into it otherwise the stain may spread. After some time remove the cloth, wring it out and dry it in the sun.

◆ Clothes stained with hair dye should be cleaned with a piece of raw onion before being washed.

◆ To remove oil stains from woollen clothes, apply a little curd over the area and wash it after some time.

◆ Oil and ghee stains can be removed from clothes, by washing in hot water to which a little washing soda has been added.

◆ To remove dirty stains from shirt collars and cuffs, dip them in cold water for an hour and scrub with sugar.

◆ To remove paint stains from glass surface, heat a teaspoon of vinegar and apply it with a piece of cloth over the stained area. The stains will vanish in no time.

◆ To remove ice-cream stains, apply a little borax powder to the spot and wash in cold water.

◆ To remove hair dye stains from garments, dip the stained portion in water. Remove from water and apply a little warm glycerine. Rub with a brush and wash well. The stain will disappear.

◆ Grease marks left on clothes will clear if scrubbed with chalk powder before immersing them in water.

◆ To remove tea or coffee stains from clothes, spray a little talcum powder over them and wash off with hot water.

◆ To remove perspiration stains from clothes, apply a little ammonia and place the dress in sunlight.

◆ Sprinkle talcum powder on ink stains before washing off with soap and water.

◆ To remove ink stains from clothes, soak them in a solution of limejuice and salt for a few minutes before washing.

◆ To remove oil stains from woollen blankets, rub the areas with curd.

◆ Stains can be removed from velvet by mixing 2 tablespoons ammonia with 2 tablespoons of warm water and rubbing this solution over the stained material with a brush. The stain will disappear within no time.

◆ Wipe leather goods with a piece of cloth soaked in warm milk to remove stains on them.

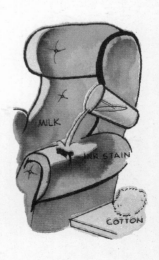

◆ Ink stains on leather covers of a sofa can be removed by pouring some milk over the stain and rubbing with clean pieces of milk-soaked cotton wool.

◆ To get rid of grease marks on wallpaper, place a blotting paper on the stain and run a hot iron over it.

◆ To remove stains from clothes, apply some glycerine over the stained area and leave it overnight. Wash in cold water, the next morning.

LIPSTICK MARKS

GLYCERINE

◆ To remove lipstick stain, apply acetone and wash with soap.

◆ Immerse white napkins, towels and handkerchiefs in a solution of washing soda and soap for 10 minutes. Stubborn stains will disappear.

◆ Rubbing a little glycerine and leaving it on for a while can remove lipstick marks. Petroleum jelly can also be used.

GARDENING

Gardening enthusiasts are always willing to experiment and share their experiences with others. The joy of consuming homegrown vegetables or seeing the flowers bloom, is something that cannot be explained. It has to be experienced. There are many hurdles to be crossed before one can reap the harvest of one's labour. The tips given here might help you to cross some of those hurdles.

◆ Empty tetrapacks can be cleaned and used as portable pots for small plants like mint, coriander and fenugreek.

◆ If ants attack ripening wall fruits, lay a band of tar mixed with a little sugar at the bottom and around tree base.

◆ To get rid of the pests from your plants, burn dry leaves and twigs in your lawn. The smoke that results from the burning will get rid of the pests.

◆ Boiling water destroys ants' nests. Boiling water poured on to weeds between pavings kills off surface leaves and retards their growth.

◆ When ants attack your plants, sprinkle a little turmeric powder around them and the ants will vanish.

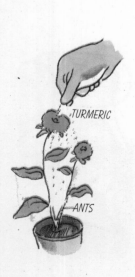

TURMERIC

ANTS

◆ Here is a recipe for home-made fertiliser - mix together superphosphate of lime, sulphate of ammonia, sulphate of potash and steamed bonemeal flour in the ratio of 7:5:2:1. Mix in water, 1-2 oz. per gallon.

◆ Make your own slug killer by mixing crushed, block methylated spirit with dry tealeaves or bran. Spread in circles around the plants to be protected.

◆ Aphids and whitefly can be kept at bay by spraying with a solution of detergent liquid and water in the same proportions as for washing dishes.

◆ Don't forget to remove and burn all diseased plants or the healthy plants may also get infected.

◆ Old net curtains make good bird deterrents when draped over soft fruit bushes or vegetable patches.

◆ Individual seed pots can be made from papier-mache egg cartons filled with potting soil.

◆ Don't throw away the ashes after the garden bonfire has cooled. You will get your own potash when you use this ash for your plants.

◆ To improve yield by retaining moisture, place well-dampened newspaper mixed with grass cuttings in the bottom of a trench being prepared for runner beans.

◆ Use '*neem*' leaves to enrich the flowerbeds instead of fertilisers.

◆ Bury your old leather boots and shoes under the soil in your garden. When they eventually rot, they add a good number of nutrients to the soil.

◆ If your garden hose has holes in it, don't throw it away. Instead, make a few more and use it as a sprinkler for your lawn or vegetable patch.

◆ For healthy indoor plants, sprinkle some gelatine powder on them, once in a month.

EPSOM SALT
+WATER

◆ For a cheap and good tonic for rose plants, add 25 gms of Epsom salt to $4\frac{1}{2}$ litres of water. Water your plants with this solution every few weeks.

◆ Crumbled eggshells make excellent calcium supplement for the potted plants.

◆ Dry tea bags and coffee powder make excellent fertiliser for your garden.

◆ To eradicate squirrels from your garden, spread mothballs all over the garden. Squirrels will not uproot the plants.

◆ Banana skins baked in an oven and buried under the soil around rose plants will give them potassium and help you get some lovely blooms.

◆ Most houseplants respond well to a light sprinkling of coffee residue on top of the soil.

◆ Pour some detergent water into the pot when you find ants attacking your plant. This will not harm the plant but will kill the ants instantly.

◆ Tonics and vitamin tablets, which have crossed their expiry date, make excellent manure for the plants, especially rose plants.

◆ Do not throw away any vegetable scrapping. Collect, dry and burn them. Use the ash as compost.

◆ Sprinkle some mustard seeds and water on soil to get rid of insects and pests.

◆ Water your plants with water to which some soda has been added. The plants will be healthier, with more foliage and flowers.

◆ Boil neem leaves in a small aluminium vessel and cool. This decoction, when sprinkled on plants, will keep pests away.

◆ Do not discard used battery cells. Break them and use the contents as manure for plants. Add plenty of water.

BATTERY CELLS

PETS

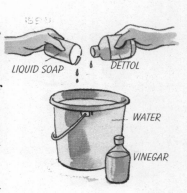

Pets have become a necessity for those who suffer from high tension and insecurity. They help in reducing the stress factors and guard the owners with their lives. In return they demand a lot of affection, love and care. The upkeep of pets can also be quite an expensive proposition. The tips given here provide low cost solutions to most of the pet problems.

◆ Make an economical anti-flea dog shampoo by mixing one part of dettol, 2 parts of liquid soap and 3 parts of water. Bottle this mixture and use whenever required. Add a tablespoon of vinegar to the water for the final rinse after every bath.

◆ Use soda bicarb as a dry shampoo and deodorant for your pet dog during the winters.

◆ If your pet dog has cracked and dry paws, rub them with a little petroleum jelly.

◆ Each time you bathe your dog, give him a final rinse with water mixed with vinegar. This controls the bad odour of wet fur.

◆ To kill the ticks that bother the pets, make a paste of *neem* leaves and apply all over the pet's body. Bathe it after a few hours.

JEWELLERY

TURMERIC POWDER

SODA BICARB

LUKEWARM WATER

A dog may be a man's best friend but as far as a woman is concerned, jewellery is her best friend. Nothing fascinates women more than a good piece of jewellery. From time immemorial, women have hoarded precious jewellery and adorned themselves with rare pieces. To own jewellery is not enough. One has to know the art of cleaning and maintaining them, too.

Cleaning and Maintenance

◆ Gold jewellery will glitter like new if you boil it in water to which a pinch of soda bicarb and a little turmeric powder has been added.

◆ Apply a coat of nail varnish over imitation jewellery to prevent it from turning black.

◆ Silver has a tendency of getting oxidized and getting tarnished. Keep your silver ornaments with a little camphor, they will not tarnish or turn black.

◆ To bring back the sparkle to your gold jewellery, apply some toothpaste on them and rub for 2-3 minutes with an old, soft toothbrush. Wash with lukewarm water.

◆ Clean the diamond jewellery with toothpaste, which has menthol in it. The jewellery will sparkle like new.

◆ To shine your silver, soak them for ½ an hour in warm water with a little sodium bi carb.

◆ Store the jewellery pieces in cloth-lined pouches, separately.

◆ Never keep pearls and diamonds together; the latter may scrape the former.

◆ Boiling jewellery for cleaning is not advisable. To wash the stubborn dirt off the gems, soak them in warm water, add a mild liquid detergent. Brush with a soft toothbrush. Rinse in hot water or alcohol. Let, dry on an absorbent towel.

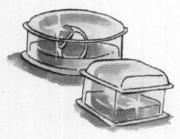

◆ A little milk added to the water used for cleaning silver will give them an extra shine.

◆ Place a few cloves in the jewellery box to absorb moisture. Moisture generally tends to tarnish most types of jewellery.

◆ Never brush diamonds with a hard toothbrush if use a soft cloth or a baby brush.

◆ Heat can cause a change in the colour of some gems. Even sunlight can change the colour of amethyst, brown to yellow topaz, kunzite and some pearls. The heat from direct sunlight can crack opals, dry up the oils used to enhance emeralds and bleach some irradiation colours and dyes.

◆ Never use household bleach with chlorine to clean studded jewellery.

◆ To keep artificial jewellery in good condition, wrap it in white tissue paper and keep in airtight container with a piece of white chalk.

◆ To clean the silver, soak a clean napkin in a mixture of 1-cup water and 1 tablespoon ammonia and 1 teaspoon silver polish. Leave the napkin to dry. Use it to remove the tarnish marks from your silver.

◆ Gold jewellery can be made to sparkle by boiling it for 2 minutes, in water to which 1 teaspoon each of turmeric powder and soap has been added.

◆ Get back the original colour of coral ornaments by applying any cooking oil to the stones and letting them dry for 2 days.

◆ The juice of white pumpkin is an effective cleanser for pearls.

◆ Gold ornaments can be cleaned with shikakai powder.

Jewellery Care

◆ **Gold:** To clean gold jewellery, wipe with a soft and clean piece of cloth. Take a little turmeric powder and apply to the jewellery and then rub gently with the cloth till the jewellery begins to shine like new.

COTTON
SWAB

Soak the gold jewellery in water to which vinegar has been added, for about an hour. With the help of a toothbrush gently brush the ornaments. Gold can also be cleaned with 'reetha' solution and sugar solution. For stone studded ornaments, wrap them in a piece of white velvet and place near steam. Rub gently to make them shine. If the gold chains get entangled, sprinkle a little talcum powder. It will then become easier to untangle the knot.

◆ **Pearls:** For cleaning pearl jewellery, rub with a cotton soaked in spirit. Rice flour can also be used to clean pearls. Care should be taken to avoid contact with water. To keep artificial pearls looking like new, keep them wrapped in cotton wool. To retain the lustre of artificial pearls, coat them with a layer of colourless nail enamel.

◆ **Diamond Studded Jewellery:** These can be cleaned with toothpaste. They can also be cleaned with 'reetha' solution. Soak the diamond studded ornaments in soap and warm water solution. Then rub with an old toothbrush to bring sheen on them. Later, soak them in alcohol and rub them dry with a piece of *mulmul* cloth.

SODA   SALT

◆ **Silver:** Take a litre of water and add a teaspoon of salt and a teaspoon of soda. Boil this solution and soak the ornaments in it. After 5 minutes take out the jewellery and immerse in a soap solution. Rub them dry with a soft material to bring a shine to them. Boil a solution of water, edible lime, juice of one lemon. Boil the silver in this solution for some time. When the solution cools, take the ornaments and rub them with an old toothbrush. If the silver has got tarnished and has black stains, take 3 glasses of water and cut 3 medium sized potatoes into it. Boil this water for about 10 minutes with the silver. The ornaments will regain their lustre and sheen.

Gem Tips

Gems which look great in combination—

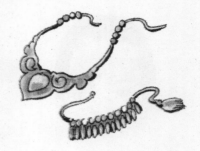

- Amethyst (purple) looks beautiful in combination with citrine or topaz (yellow).

- Garnet (maroon) is beautiful in league with topaz or citrine (yellow), as well as Peridot (light green).

- Citrine or Topaz with Lolite (purplish blue).

- Amethyst with peridot.

- Aquamarine (very light blue) with amethyst (purple).

While setting—

- Best set in silver—Lapis Lazuli (deep blue), Black Onyx, Turquoise, Garnet, Amethyst, and all opaque stones.

- Diamonds set in white gold, gold plated with radium or platinum look much more attractive as the prongs do not show as much as the yellow gold ones. Jewellery set in this manner gives the illusion that there are more diamonds in it.

- Since 18 carat gold is a tougher metal to hold stones, it is advisable to use it for making gem studded jewellery.

- Darker stones always look better when set with diamonds.

- If the jewellery setting is with diamonds, don't use too many coloured gems.

- If mixing coloured gems for a piece of jewellery, don't use two dark shades, they will look lustre-less.

- All jewellery settings have to be done in such a way that the gemstone captures light.

- Emerald is a brittle stone, so it's setting is not recommended in jewellery, which will face regular wear and tear. There are less chances of it breaking when used in earrings and pendants.

- Wear jewellery according to your personality. If you have large hands, chunky bracelets and rings will look good on them. But if your hands are delicate looking, you should go in for dainty designs. If you

have broad shoulders, chunky necklaces and thick chains will look good, but if they are narrow, only fragile looking ones will do.

◆ The size of your ears - if you have large ears, use earrings which will cover a part of them, but for small ears, large earrings are a taboo.

◆ For short hair, earrings should be worn close to the ear to give a flattering look.

◆ Round, hooped earrings will not look good on a big, fat face.

◆ Chokers help to cover a part of the neck so people with long necks look good with them while a short neck looks still stumpier with a choker.

Traditional Rules for Wearing Gems

Indians have always believed in the power of gems. It is believed that gems can ward off evil, bring happiness and prosperity and keep a person healthy. Astrologers always advise that gems should be worn for different kinds of benefits but they also specify how the gems should be worn. There are several traditional rules for wearing gems. Here are some of them:

The entire left side of your body, arm, hand and fingers, receive energy from outside. When you wear certain gems on your left side, you can consciously control and modify stress from your environment. On the other hand, gems when worn on the right side of the body, aid productivity.

Index finger—they are your directional fingers of expression and a gem on these can influence your communication, goals, dreams and desires. On your left finger, stones aid inner communication. When worn on the right, they can assist in sharing their energy towards directed actions.

Middle finger—the middle finger is intuitive and inspirational. Wear a ring on it when you want to stimulate your inspiration.

LEMON JUICE

CLUB SODA

Ring finger—the ring finger on the left hand is a creative finger. Gems worn on the left ring finger receive creative stimulation even in love, hence the wedding band.

Little finger—if you want a change or opportunity, wear gems on the little finger of your left hand. It will aid you in accepting changes. On the right little finger, it will influence the change of fortunes or goals.

Gem Cures

Red coral and emerald can cure you of all gallstones; a blue sapphire can rid you of asthma. A large size pearl is good for menstrual problems. The measure of the intensity of energy is very important. Each gem has its own exclusive, radioactive energy. For instance, sapphire has titanium in it. When a stone touches the body, the energy passes through the skin to the blood and in the process reaches the brain.

Each gem has an atomic arrangement, it is either 8,6, or 4 sided and in their purest form, the gems are colourless. Every gem has traces of elements like copper, iron, titanium and gives colours to itself, which results in different radiations. The cosmic rays pass through the angles of the crystalline form of the precious stones with a hardness varying from 1-10. The gems should be radiated naturally. Irradiated gemstones can have a bad effect on one's body.

Sometimes gems are reduced to powder, and dissolved, as far as possible, in water or some liquid and taken internally. Homeopaths soak gemstones like diamonds in pure alcohol and mix it with their medicines. Powdered pearls are added to a mixture of rose water and *amla* and consumed during summer. This is said to give a cooling effect to the body.

Some Popular Gem Prescriptions

Emeralds and *Gomeda* (hessonite)—to prevent gastric troubles and acidity.

Red corals and pearls—to prevent accidents.

Red corals and topaz—to prevent anaemia.

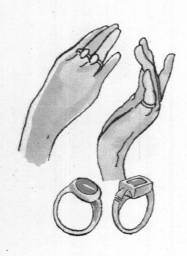

Blue sapphire—to prevent asthma.

Red coral and yellow sapphire—to treat arthritis.

Red corals—for bronchitis, colds and constipation.

Light blue sapphire and red corals—to prevent cancer.

Red coral and yellow sapphire—for diabetes.

Red coral and emerald—for ENT problems.

Diamond and topaz—for eczema.

Emerald and pearls—for epilepsy.

Emerald, topaz, pearl and ruby—for heart ailments.

Emerald, topaz and blue sapphire—for high blood pressure.

Red coral and pearls—for hysteria.

Emerald, pearl and topaz—for insomnia.

Emerald and topaz—for indigestion.

Red coral and blue sapphire—for jaundice.

Emerald, diamond and topaz—for mental deficiency.

Large sized pearl—for menstrual problems.

Red coral and emerald—for paralysis.

Red coral and topaz—for tuberculosis.

Emerald, topaz and pearl—for typhoid.

Birthstones

January—Garnet

February—Amethyst

March—Jasper

April—Sapphire

May—Carnelian, Agate

June—Emerald

July—Onyx

August—Carnelian

September—Chrysolite

October—Aquamarine

November—Topaz

December—Ruby

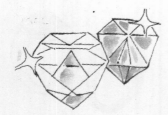

PRACTICAL TIPS

Most of the times it is the practical and common sense, which guides us through the various problems we face in our day-to-day living. However, common sense doesn't seem to be so common, these days. The hints listed under this head are meant to be of help in various situations that baffle us in our everyday life.

◆ Used mosquito mats make excellent blotting agents.

◆ Mustard oil is an excellent anti-rust agent for all types of iron surfaces.

◆ While steam-ironing clothes, add a few drops of cologne or perfume to the water, for a lingering fragrance.

◆ Wear latex gloves while opening jars, for a slip-free grip.

◆ If the toothpaste tube is difficult to squeeze, keep the tube on a wooden board and press it from back to front with a '*chapati* roller'.

◆ What do you do when a glass breaks and scatters all over the floor? It is dangerous to leave even a single piece as it may injure someone. Use damp cotton wool to gather broken pieces of glass from the floor.

◆ If the cap of a bottle has become loose, tie a string around the neck and fit the cap on it.

◆ Dip the ends of shoelaces in melted candle wax and roll between fingers and thumb for a neat finish. This will also prevent them from fraying.

◆ To straighten crumpled plastic sheets or packets cover them with cotton cloth and run a warm iron over them.

◆ If you are planning for a party, start collecting ice cubes in plastic bags 2-3 days in advance so that you don't have to run to the neighbours at the last minute.

◆ To elongate the life of cut flowers in a vase, add salt to the water. You could also add a tablet of aspirin for the same effect.

- Add a little sugar and liquid detergent to the water in a flower vase. The sugar will help retain the freshness of the flowers and the detergent will not allow the water to turn stale.

- An old toothbrush is invaluable in removing dirt and old paint from carvings, etc.

- To make a handy funnel, cut through an empty mineral water bottle, about 4" down from the neck.

- Do you want the doors to open smoothly and noiselessly? Here is what you can do to stop doors from creaking. Put a little talcum powder over the hinges.

- During monsoon, the address on a postal envelope can be made waterproof by rubbing a candle over it.

- Sprinkle a little baking powder in the ashtray to prevent the smoke from spreading.

- To counteract the monsoon humidity effects on your carpet, place a layer of newspaper under them.

- Use dental floss or plastic thread to sew buttons on kids' clothes. They will hold for a long time.

- If your child finds the taste of a certain medicine unpalatable, ask her to suck on an ice cube before drinking the medicine. The cold chills the taste buds and the child will drink the medicine without any fuss. Don't try this when the child has fever or cold.

- To remove postage stamps, which stick together, cover with a wet cloth and iron lightly.

- Add a little coal powder or salt to the water in a flower vase. The flowers remain fresh for a longer time, this way.

- When there is a hole in the mosquito net, seal it with an adhesive tape to prevent it from getting bigger.

- Stop grappling with the rusted nuts and bolts. Pour club soda over rusty nuts and bolts, to loosen them.

- When albums get old, photos tend to stick to the album and look patchy. If you dip cotton wool in petrol and wipe the photos, they will regain their original shine.

CASTOR OIL

COCONUT OIL

◆ To prevent coconut oil from freezing during the winter, add 8-10 drops of castor oil to it.

◆ To avoid shoe bites, apply sour curd, wherever the shoe is pinching, and let it act overnight. Just wipe off the curd, the shoe will be soft.

◆ To identify your suitcase from a distance, on the conveyer belt, tie a coloured satin or silk ribbon on its handle.

◆ To remove rust from needles or pins, pierce them in a cake of soap 3-4 times.

◆ Empty soft drink cans can be used as ashtrays and discarded after they are full.

◆ Shopping bags and knick-knacks can be made out of old plastic bags. Cut them into even strips and plait three strips at a time to make a thick cord that can be sewn into different shapes for making telephone mats, coasters, dining table mats etc. With wool, crochet hook, crochet a shopping bag and the handle. Crochet the handle, button and loop separately and fix on to the bag. Embellish the bag with crochet roses and leaves.

◆ If the ball pen stops writing, rub the nib on a piece of glass. It will start working immediately.

◆ Melt and spread the wax drippings, from candles, on the floor before placing your gas cylinder over it. The floor will not get stained.

◆ Add ½ a tablet of Dispirin to the flower vase, the flowers remain fresh for a longer time.

◆ Cellophane tape stuck on the edges of children's books prevents the pages from tearing accidentally.

◆ Sprinkle sand on wet paint while painting a ladder. This makes the ladder slip proof.

◆ Rub candle wax over the address written in ink, on a parcel. This will prevent the address from getting washed off during the rainy season.

- Use old greeting cards for making colourful collage, for bedroom walls. They can be cut and made into beautiful bookmarks, too.

- Postage stamps, which are stuck together, can be separated easily by putting them in the fridge for a few minutes.

- Applying pencil lead or rubbing with a small piece of soap can silence creaking hinges.

- To find the elusive loose end of the cello tape, place the roll in the fridge for about 10 minutes.

- Lace curtains and nets will stiffen and shine if they are given a final rinse in water to which methylated spirit has been added.

- To make the curtains non- inflammable, give them a final rinse in a bucket of water containing 50 gm of alum.

- Add a few drops of castrol oil to the coconut oil bottle to prevent the oil from thickening, during winter.

- Stick a square piece of sandpaper on the inside lid of your child's pencil box. It comes handy for cleaning dirty erasers.

- To retain the heat in a hot water bottle or bag, add a pinch of salt to the water. The water remains hot for a longer time.

- If the gum has dried up, add a little vinegar to it.

- Immersing nails in water before hammering them into the walls will prevent the plaster from falling off.

- Mix a few grams of baking soda in a packet of white cement and make a thin liquid paste. Pour this slowly into cracks in the roof. This will totally plug them and prevent water from leaking into the house.

- To darn a pair of socks, place an electric bulb inside it.

- Sharpen a blunt needle by running it through sandpaper half a dozen times

Gadget Tips

◆ Dab a little eau-de-cologne on cotton wool and use it to clean your tape recorder head.

◆ Rum can also be used to clean the head of a tape recorder.

◆ If the audiocassette makes a scratching noise, keep it in the freezer for five minutes and the noise will disappear.

◆ To clean dirty electric switches, clean them with a cloth dipped in kerosene.

◆ For a sparkling clean car, wear an old socks or two on your hands and clean.

◆ To prevent a car windscreen from freezing on an icy morning, rub it with a cut potato.

◆ Increase the life of the car wipers during monsoon by rubbing them with sand paper.

◆ Line the car floor with a double lining of mats and waterproof covering, to keep them from absorbing moisture during the monsoon.

◆ If you are fed up with the loud noise your fridge makes, each time the motor starts up, look for the imbalance. The rattling sound made due to vibrations can be set right if the position is adjusted.

◆ All electric appliances, which emanate heat, should be kept away from the wall. Leave a space of at least 2 feet from the wall, while placing the fridge, television, computer and music system.

◆ To make the overstretched sewing machine belts taut once again, place them in cold water for 30 minutes and dry in strong sun.

◆ Apply petroleum jelly (vaseline) to the rubber valve in the flush tank if it leaks.

◆ To keep an electric iron from rusting, rub a little olive oil on it while it is still warm.

EAU-DE-COLOGNE

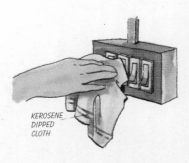

KEROSENE DIPPED CLOTH

Eco-Friendly Substitutes

AMMONIA — BAKING SODA

As awareness is awakening in people, the realization that we cannot take the natural resources for granted is also surfacing. The need of the hour is to find eco-friendly substitutes for all the synthetic and chemical things that we are using for various purposes. Each of us can do our little bit for the environment and if each person does his bit, it will make a huge difference to the world we live in. Here is a list of some substitute that can be easily used in most homes.

◆ Drain cleaners - pour boiling water down the drain a couple of times a week as a preventive measure followed by ½ cup baking soda and ½ cup vinegar and 4 cups of boiling water.

◆ Oven cleaners—ammonia or baking soda.

◆ Toilet bowl cleaners—baking soda, mild detergent

◆ Copper cleaners—vinegar and salt

◆ Furniture polish—mineral oil with lime juice

◆ Powder cleaners—baking soda, non-bleach containing powders

◆ Window cleaners—vinegar and water, dry with newspaper

◆ Chlorine bleach—baking soda and water

◆ Mothballs—neem leaves

◆ Mildew removers—equal portions of vinegar and salt

◆ Air fresheners—simmer cinnamon and cloves in water.

◆ Spot removers—rinse immediately with cold water, club soda and lemon juice.

◆ Silver polish—soak silver in water with baking soda and salt and then wipe dry. Polish with toothpaste.

For Your Car

Here are some tips to for maintaining your car—

◆ Turmeric can seal a hole in a very efficient manner. Use it to plug a leaking radiator.

◆ If you smear grease on to the headlights, it will improve the visibility while driving through fog.

◆ A couple of cigarettes, when rubbed on the windscreen can make the wipers work smoothly.

◆ Loose cables on the battery can be fixed by jamming a matchstick or a toothpick between the cables and the terminal.

Soapy Tricks

◆ If you thought that soap is only for washing or for having your bath, think again. Here are some interesting uses for the ordinary soap.

◆ Lifebuoy soap can be used for a car, too. Rub it on a hole in the fuel tank to prevent leakage.

◆ Rubbing soap on the exact spot of the leak can stop it temporarily.

◆ And if you rub a cake of soap on the dry windscreen and lather it, you will be surprised to note the clarity of vision even when the wiper blade is worn out.

Annexure

Calorie Content of Common Food Items in Convenient Measures

A. Raw Foods

Item	Measure	Weight g.	Energy Cal.	Item	Measure	Weight g.	Energy Cal.
Cereals Rice	1 Cup (small)	150	520	Coconut (fresh)	1 no.	115	510
				Coconut (dry)	1/2 no.	45	290
Wheat flour	"	90	310	Groundnuts	50 no.	15	85
Millet Flour	"	90	300	Sesame seeds	1 tsp.	3	15
Pulses Bengal gram	"	130	485	Oils/Vanaspati ghee	2 tsp.	10 ml.	100
				Spices Chilli powder	1 tsp.	7	17
Other dals	"	135	460	Coriander seeds	1 tsp.	7	20
Whole Pulses Greengram	"	140	470	Cumin seeds	1 tsp.	5	18
Cowpea (lobia)	"	135	440	Fenugreek (Methi)	1 tsp.	6	20
Rajma	"	120	415	Mustard seeds	1 tsp.	10	5
Soyabean	"	130	530	Garlic	7 pods	3	4
Green leafy vegetables	5 Bundles	100	62	Onion	1 med.	50	30
				Animal foods Egg (hen)	One	60	100
Other vegetables		100	105	Mutton		100	194
Nuts and Oilseeds Almonds	10 no.	15	85	Fish (lean)		100	100
Cashewnuts	10 no.	15	95	Fish (fatty)		100	150

Notes: tsp: teaspoon (5 ml.), **tbsp:** table spoon (15 ml.), **1 cup (small)** = 150 ml.

B. Cooked Foods

Item	No. of Serving	Weight gms.	Energy cal.	Item	No. of Serving	Weight gms.	Energy cal.
Cereal preparations Rice	1 Cup	100	110	Dahi vada	1	80	170
Idli	"	60	75	Vegetable cutlet	1	30	70
Plain dosa	"	40	125	**Chutneys**			
Masala dosa	"	100	200	Coconut/ground nuts/til/coriander	1tbsp	25	64
Phulka	"	35	80	Tomato	1 tbsp	20	10
Paratha	"	50	150	**Non-Vegetarian preparations**			
Upma	"	130	200	Boiled egg	1	50	86
Sevian upma	"	80	130	Omelette	1	65	155
Bread toasted	2 slices	50	170	Fried egg	1	50	155
Poha (Awal)	1 Cup	100	200	Mutton curry	1 cup	145	240
Dalia	"	140	165	Chicken curry	"	125	260
Khichidi	"	100	210	Fish (fried)	2 pieces	85	220
Puri	1	25	80	**Bakery products**			
Pulse preparations Plain dal	1 Cup	140	170	Biscuits	2	40	220
Sambhar	"	160	81	Cake	1	40	220
Chole/Sundal	"	150	115	Vegetable puff	1	60	170
Vegetable preparations With gravy	1 Cup	130	130	Pastry	1	50	350
				Mathri	2	75	300
Dry	"	100	115	**Sweets**			
Bagara Baigan	"	170	230	Laddu, burfi etc.	1	60	250
Vegetable kofta	"	145	220	Halwa (Suji)	1 cup	130	430
Fried snacks Bhaji	1	7	35	Double ka meetha	"	105	280
				Custard/puddings	"	110	180
Samosa	1	65	210	Chikki	2	60	300
Kachori	1	45	200	Jam/Jelly	1tsp.	7	20
Potato Bonda	1	40	100	Sugar	1 tbsp	15 ml.	20
Sago vada	1	30	100	Honey	1 tbsp	15 ml.	60
Masala vada	1	20	56	Jalebi	2 pieces	100 gm.	500
Vada	1	20	65	Gulab Jamun	"	50 gm.	400
				Jaggery	1 tbsp.	15 gm.	56

C. Salads			
Item	No.	Weight gms.	Energy cal.
Beetroot	1	65	30
Cabbage	1	250	70
Carrot	1	40	20
Cucumber	1	90	12
Lettuce	6 bundles	100	20
Onion	1	50	25
Radish	1	60	10
Tomato	1	50	10
Turnip	1	100	30

D. Fruits			
Item	No./ Quantity	Weight gms.	Energy cal.
Apple	1	100	65
Banana	1	80	90
Grapes	30	100	70
Guava	1	100	50
Jackfruit	4 pieces	100	90
Mango	1	250	180
Mosambi/orange	1	100	40
Papaya	1 piece	250	80
Pineapple	1 piece	100	50
Sapota	1	80	80
Custard apple	1	130	130
Watermelon/ Muskmelon	1 piece	100	15

E. Beverages			
Item	Measure	Qty. ml.	Energy cal.
Coffee	1 cup	150	100
Tea	1 cup	150	60
Carbonated beverages	1 bottle	200	150
Fresh lime juice	1 glass	200	60
Squash	"	200	80
Syrups (sherbat)	"	200	200
Orange juice	"	200	150

F. Milk and Milk Products			
Item	Measure	Qty. ml.	Energy cal.
Milk (Buffalo)	1 cup	150 ml.	300
Milk (cow)	"	150 ml.	100
Curd (cow)	"	150 ml.	85
Buttermilk (lassi)	"	150 ml.	45
Paneer	"	100 gm.	350
Ghee	2 tsp	10 ml.	100
Butter	3 tsp	15 ml.	100
Khoya (from whole milk)		100 gm.	400
Khoya (Butter separated)		100 gm.	200
Skimmed milk	1 cup	150 ml.	45
Cream	1 tbsp	15 ml.	50
Cheese	1 packet	30 gm.	100
Rabadi	1 cup	150 gm.	525

Cholesterol Content of Animal Foods

Item	Fat g/100 g.	Saturated fatty acids g/100 g.	Choles- terol mg/100 g.	Item	Fat g/100 g.	Saturated fatty acids g/100 g.	Choles- terol mg/100g.
Butter	80	50	250	Beef	16	8	70
Ghee	100	65	300	Mutton	13	7	65
Milk (cow)	4	2	14	Pork	35	13	90
Milk (buffalo)	8	4	16	**Organ meats**			
Milk (skimmed)	0.1	-	2	Brain	6	2	2000
Milk (condensed)	10	6	40	Heart	5	2	150
Cream	13	8	40	Kidney	2	1	370
Cheese	25	15	100	Liver	9	3	300
Egg (whole)	11	4	400	**Sea foods**			
Egg yolk	30	9	1120	Prawns/shrimps	2	0.3	150
Chicken without skin	4	1	60	Fish (lean)	1.5	0.4	45
Chicken with skin	18	6	100	Fish (fatty)	6	2.5	45

NUTRITIVE VALUE OF FOODS

(Amounts given per 100 gms of edible portion)

Food	Water ml	Calories	Protein gm	Fat gm	Carbo-hydrate	Fibre gm	Calcium mg	Iron mg	Vit. A i.u.	B1 mg	B2 mg	Niacin mg	Vit. C mg
1	2	3	4	5	6	7	8	9	10	11	12	13	14
Almond	5	657	20	59	12	1.7	230	4.5	—	.3	.6	4.5	—
Amla	81	55	0.5	.10	14	3.4	50	1.2	—	—	—	—	600
Animal fat	1	891	—	99	—	—	—	—	—	—	—	—	—
Apple	84	61	.3	.4	14	1	4	1	20	.02	.04	.2	5
Apricot	90	36	1	—	8	.4	15	1	2000	.03	.05	.5	5
Bajra millet	13	361	11.6	.5	67.5	1.2	42	5	—	.33	.25	2.3	—
Banana	70	116	1	.3	27	.3	7	.5	100	.1	.08	.8	7
Barley	13	336	22.5	1.3	62.6	3.9	26	8	—	.47	.20	5.4	—
Bathua leaves	90	30	3.7	.4	2.9	.8	150	4.2	—	.01	.14	.6	35
Beetroot	87	45	1.8	—	10	.7	15	1	—	.02	.03	3	5
Black pepper	13	347	12	7	59	4.9	130	10	—	.04	.2	1	—
Brown Khandsari	1	389	.2	—	97	—	30	2	—	0.2	.1	.3	—
Butter	16	745	.5	82.5	—	—	15	.2	3000	—	—	—	—
Butter oil pure	8	828	—	92	—	—	—	—	2000	—	—	—	—
Cane juice	81	73	.3	—	18	—	6	2	—	.02	.02	.1	10
Cardamom dried	20	228	10	2	43	20	113	5	—	—	—	—	—
Carrot	90	33	1	—	7	.8	40	.7	3000	.05	.05	.5	.6
Cashewnut	5	590	20	45	26	1.3	50	5	—	.6	.2	2.1	—
Cauliflower	90	33	3	.2	5	1	30	1	20	.1	.1	.7	—
Cumin seed	12	356	19	15	36	12	1080	31	300	—	—	2.6	—
Cinnamon	12	229	12	7.8	28	35	440	17	—	.1	.4	2.4	—
Clove	23	293	5	9	48	10	740	5	—	.1	.2	2	—
Coconut Kernel	20	375	4	35	11	4	10	2	—	.05	.02	.6	—
Cucumber	96	12	.6	—	2	.5	15	.3	—	.04	.02	.2	10
Custard apple	75	93	1	—	22	1	25	.5	—	.1	.08	.8	30
Dried dates	20	303	2	—	74	2.4	70	2	50	.07	.05	2	—
Dried pea	10	337	25	1	57	4.5	70	5	100	.8	.2	2.5	—
Eggplant (brinjal)	93	22	1.	—	4	1	10	1	—	.05	.03	.8	5
Fig-dried	20	269	4	—	63	11	200	4	100	.1	.08	1.7	—
Fig-fresh	85	49	1.3	—	11	2	50	1	80	.05	.05	.4	2
Fresh beans & peas	70	104	7	—	19	2.5	40	15	500	.3	.15	1.5	25
Fresh mushroom	91	13	2.5	.3	—	1	20	1	—	.12	.5	5.8	3
Garlic	63	139	6	—	29	.8	13	1.3	—	.25	.08	.4	10
Gourd	92	28	.7	—	6	.3	20	.6	—	.04	.03	.6	15
Gram, whole	10	338	22	.5	61	5.3	280	8	40	.4	.15	2.5	—
Mung bean (Green)	12	324	22	1	57	4.7	100	8	40	.45	.2	2	—
Grape	80	76	1	—	18	.5	20	.3	50	.04	.02	.3	5

Food	Water ml	Calories	Protein gm	Fat gm	Carbo-hydrate	Fibre gm	Calcium mg	Iron mg	Vit. A i.u.	B1 mg	B2 mg	Niacin mg	Vit. C mg
1	2	3	4	5	6	7	8	9	10	11	12	13	14
Groundnut	6	579	27	45	17	3	50	2.5	—	.9	.15	17	—
Guava	80	58	1	.4	13	5.5	15	1	200	.05	.04	1	200
Honey	23	286	4	—	76	—	5	.4	—	—	.05	.2	—
Jam	29	260	.4	—	69	.6	12	.3	—	—	—	—	10
Lemon	85	55	1.1	0.9	11.1	1.7	70	2.3	—	—	—	—	39
Lettuce	94	19	1.4	—	3	.5	35	2.4	300 2000	.1	.1	.4	15
Litchi	82	71	.9	.5	16	.3	5	.5	—	.04	.04	.3	50
Lobia bean	12	323	24.1	1	54.5	3.8	77	5.9	60	.51	.2	1.3	—
(black kidney bean)	11	329	24	1	56	4.5	150	9	40	.4	.2	2	—
Maize, whole	12	363	10	4.5	71	2	12	2.5	—	.35	.13	2	—
Mango	83	63	.5	—	15	.8	10	.5	600	.03	.04	.3	30
Mustard leaves	85	34	4	.6	3.2	.8	155	16.3	—	.03	—	—	33
Melon seeds (without cover)	6	581	25	45	19	2	50	8	—	.2	.15	1.5	—
Methi leaves	85	49	4.4	.9	6	1.1	395	16.5	—	.04	.31	.8	52
Musk-melon	93	26	.5	—	6	.4	10	.4	500	.03	.03	.5	30
Orange, Malta	86	53	.8	—	13	.3	30	.5	30	.08	.03	.2	45
Papaya	89	39	.8	—	9	.7	20	.5	1000	.03	.03	.2	50
Peach	85	56	.8	—	13	.5	8	.5	300	.02	.03	.3	10
Pear	84	59	.3	—	15	.9	7	.4	—	.02	.02	.2	4
Pineapple	85	57	.4	—	14	.5	20	.5	100	.08	.03	.1	30
Pistachio	6	626	20	54	15	2	140	14	100	7	.5	1.5	—
Plum	88	45	.7	—	11	.4	10	.4	30	.02	.03	.3	5
Pomegranate	80	77	1	—	18	.2	3	.7	—	.02	.02	.2	8
Potato	80	75	2	—	17	.4	10	.7	—	.1	.03	1.5	15
Pumpkin seeds (without cover)	4	610	30	50	10	2	40	10	30	.2	.2	2	—
Radish	94	18	1	—	4	.7	30	1	—	.03	.03	.3	25
Red kidney bean	12	346	22.9	1.3	60.6	4.5	260	5.8	60	—	—	—	—
Rice, lightly milled	12	354	8	1.5	77	.5	10	2	—	.25	.05	2	—
Sorghum, Jawar	12	353	10	2.5	73	1.5	20	4	—	.4	.1	3	—
Soyabean	8	382	35	18	20	4.5	200	7-11	—	1.1	.3	2	—
Spinach	85	48	5	.7	5	1.5	250	10.9	3000	.1	.3	1.5	100
Sugar white	—	400	—	—	100	—	—	—	—	—	—	—	—
Sweet Lemon (Mosambi)	84.6	55	1.5	1.0	10.9	1.3	90	.3	26	.04	—	.2	63
Sweet potato	70	114	1.5	.3	26	1	25	1	100	.1	.04	.7	30
Tamarind	20	304	2	—	74	2	50	3	50	.4	.15	1.5	10
Tomato	94	20	1	—	4	.6	5	.4	250	.06	.04	.7	25
Turnip	90	34	1	—	8	.7	30	.4	—	.06	.04	.7	25
Walnut	3	697	15	65	13	2.1	80	2	—	.4	.1	.7	—
Wheat flour, whole	13	341	10	1	75	—	16	1.5	—	.08	.05	.8	—
Wheat sprouted	13	397	29.2	7.4	53.3	1.4	40	6	—	1.4	.54	2.9	—
Wheat, whole	13	344	11.5	2	70	2	30	3.5	—	.4	.1	5	—
Yam	73	104	2	.2	24	.5	10	1.2	20	.1	.03	.4	10

SAMPLE BALANCED DIET CHARTS

Table-1: Diet (containing 1200 calories)

Morning	:		One cup of tea or coffee (without sugar)
Breakfast	:	1.	2 bread pieces, or dalia 35 gms. or cheese 30 gms, or one egg.
		2.	One cup of milk
		3.	One fruit - Guava, Mosambi, Orange or Apple
Lunch	:	1.	One chapati 20 gms.
		2.	Rice half katori, or one chapati
		3.	Dal one katori
		4.	Vegetable one katori
		5.	'Mattha' (buttermilk) one katori, or dahi half katori
		6.	One cucumber, or radish
Evening	:	1.	One cup of tea
		2.	Two namkeen biscuits, or upma half katori, or roasted grams (chana) 50 gms.
Dinner	:	1.	Two chapatis
		2.	Dal one katori
		3.	Vegetable one katori
		4.	'Mattha' one katori, or dahi half katori
		5.	One cucumber, or radish, or carrot
Oil or ghee	:		Three teaspoonful of oil (15 gms) in the whole day for cooking only

Table-2: Diet (containing 1500 calories)

Morning	:	Lemon water/tea/coffee without sugar
Breakfast	:	Bread two pieces, or dalia 40 gms, or one chapati & butter 5 gms (one teaspoonful)
Between 10-11 O' clock	:	Lemon water/mattha/tea or coffee without sugar
Lunch	:	Two ordinary chapatis (20 gms.) Dal one katori Dahi one katori Green vegetable, salad 250 gms, one fruit
Evening	:	One cup of tea without sugar Two namkeen biscuits
Dinner		Two ordinary chapatis Meat/fish/chicken (100 gms), or cheese (60 gms), or dal one katori, Green vegetable, or salad One fruit
Before going to bed	:	Milk one glass without sugar
Oil or Ghee	:	Three teaspoons in a day (that will be used in cooking)

Table-3: Diet (containing 1800 calories)

Morning	:	One cup of tea
Breakfast	:	One cup of milk Bread piece two, or dalia 35 gms, or an egg or cheese 30 gms.
At 11'O clock	:	One cup of tea
Lunch	:	3 Chapatis (60 gms.) Dal (30 gms.), or chicken (40 gms.) Dahi 75 gms. Vegetable one katori
Evening	:	One cup of tea Two namkeen biscuits, or 50 gm roasted chana
Dinner	:	3 Chapatis (60 gms.) Dal 30 gm (one katori) Meat or cheese 40 gms. Vegetable one katori
At 9'O clock at night	:	One cup of milk
Oil or ghee	:	20 gm in a whole day for cooking

Table-4: Diet (containing 2200 calories)

Morning	:	One cup of tea (without sugar)
Breakfast	:	Milk 250 ml. (Brown bread 2 pieces, or dalia 60 gms, or an egg, or cheese 30 gms.
Lunch	:	4 Chapatis (80 gms.) Dal one katori, or peas (40 gms.) Dahi one katori Vegetable two katories
Evening	:	One cup of tea Two namkeen biscuits
Dinner	:	4 Chapatis Dal one katori Cheese (40 gms.) Vegetable one katori
Before going to bed	:	One cup of milk
Oil or ghee	:	25 gms in a whole day for cooking

Notes :
Nutrient Guidelines for balanced diet.

1. For a balanced diet, your diet should consist of the appropriate quantity from each of the following food groups:
   - **Cereals/Bread:** Rice, chapatis, bread and other cereals like suji etc.
   - Fruits & vegetables.
   - Meat, fish, eggs or vegetable protein foods (legumes, pulses).
   - **Dairy products:** Milk, cheese, curd.
   - **Oils & Fats:** Butter, oil, ghee.
2. Calories should be sufficient to maintain appropriate body weight for a given height.
3. Total fat intake should be between 15-30% of total calories.
4. Proteins should provide around 10-15% of calories.
5. Carbohydrates should constitute 55-65% of calories with emphasis on complex carbohydrates.
6. If you take protein, carbohydrate & fat in the following manner, the requirement under point 3, 4 & 5 will automatically suffice—
   - Protein: 1 gm/kg of body weight.
   - Fat: 1 gm/kg of body weight.
   - Carbohydrate: 4 to 7 gm/kg of body weight.
7. Cholesterol should not exceed 300 mg/day in the diet. A cholesterol free diet is preferable.
8. Saturated fat(s) should be less than 8% of total calories.
9. Polyunsaturated fat (P) should not exceed 10% of total calories.
10. S/P ratio should be between 0.8 - 1.0.
11. Linoleic Acid (LA) should range between 3-7% of calories.
12. Alpha-Linolenic Acid (ALNA) should not be less than 1% of calories (Refer Table 15 for clarification)
13. LA/ALNA ratio should be between 5-10.
14. Sugar should be less than 10% of total calories and should be kept to a minimum.
15. Salt intake should be between 5-7 g/day.
16. Dietary fibre should be around 40 g/day.

CHART FOR HEALTHY HEART

Foods	Prefer	Limit (reduce)	Avoid
Cereals	wheat, rice, ragi, bajra, maize jowar	foods prepared with maida like white bread & biscuit	cakes, pastries, naan roti, roomali roti, noodles.
Pulses	whole & sprouted dals	—	—
Vegetables	green leafy vegetables and other vegetables	roots and tubers	fried vegetables, banana chips, canned vegetables
Fruits	fresh fruits		dried fruits, canned fruits in syrup
Dairy products	low fat milk, buttermilk, skimmed milk	full-cream milk, milk powders	cheese, butter, khoya, condensed milk, cream
Eggs	egg white	—	egg yolk
Animal foods	fish	chicken	prawns, shrimps, all types of meat
Fat	more than one type of vegetable oil	total fat intake	oily dishes, butter, ghee coconut oil, vanaspati, deep-fried foods
Sugar & sugar products	jaggery	sugar in any home-made beverages	sweets like chocolates, icecreams
Nuts & oilseeds		all nuts & oilseeds	
Beverages	fresh fruit juice (without sugar), light tea	coffee, cola, soft drinks	alcohol
Salt	foods in natural state	too much salt in preparations	pickles, papads, sauces, salt biscuits, fried crispies

WEIGHT AND MEASURES

Weight and measures are given for your general guidance. Once you become familiar with the art of cooking, you could use guessed quantities of ingredients and churn out delicious recipes.

Conversion Tables for Weights

Imperial (in ounces)	Metric [in gms (approx.)]
1	25
2	50
3	75
4 ($^1/_4$ lb)	100
6	175
8 ($^1/_2$ lb)	225
10	275
16 (1 lb)	450
18	500
35	1000 (1 kg)

Liquid Measures

Imperial	Metric [in ml (approx.)]
1 tsp	5
1 tbsp	15
2 tbsps	30
10 tbsps (1/4 pint)	150
20 tbsps (1/2 pint)	300
1 pint	600
$1^3/_4$ pints	1000 (1 ltr)
1 cup	210

PS: Use one set of measurements throughought your recipe.

A BACKGROUND ABOUT FLOUR KNEADING

The Indian equivalent to the western bread are the traditional phulka, paratha, puri, luchi among others. Atta and maida are first kneaded with water and salt into doughs of varying stiffness. Sometimes the dough is kneaded along with some vegetables or boiled pulses or spices to make them delicious and wholesome. The kneaded dough is then put through different processes of baking, shallow frying or deep frying before consumption. The following table will give you an idea about the ingredients that go into the preparation of the Indian breads and the way they are cooked.

S. No.	Food item/Qty.	Ingredients used	Cooked on
1.	Roti (2)	1 cup atta, $^1/_2$ cup water, $^1/_4$ tsp salt	Tawa
2.	Paratha (3)	1 cup atta, 2 tbsp ghee/oil, $^1/_4$ tsp salt, $^1/_2$ cup water	Shallow fried on a tawa
3.	Tandoori roti (2)	1 cup atta, $^1/_2$ tsp salt, a pinch baking soda, 2 tbsp ghee/oil, water	Baked in a clay tandoor
4.	Naan (4)	2 cups maida, warm water, 1 tsp dahi, $^1/_2$ tbsp dry yeast, sugar, 2 tbsp ghee/oil	Baked in a clay tandoor
5.	Puri (6)	1 cup atta, 2 tbsp ghee/oil, $^1/_4$ tsp salt, water	Deep fried in a karahi
6.	Bhature (6)	2 cups maida, dahi $^1/_2$ cup, $^1/_2$ cup warm water $^1/_2$ tsp salt, $^1/_2$ tsp baking powder, 1 tbsp ghee/oil	Deep fried in a karahi
7.	Luchi (6)	1 cup maida, 2 tsp ghee/oil, $^1/_2$ tsp salt, $^1/_2$ cup water	Deep fried in a karahi

VACCINATION TABLE FOR CHILDREN

S. No. Disease	Vaccine/Medicine	First Time	Second Time	Third Time
1. Tetanus	Tetanus Toxide	To mother during pregnancy	+++	+++
2. Tuberculosis	B.C.G.	One month after birth	At the age of 5 years	+++
3. Small-pox	Vaccine	Upto age of 3 months	At the age of 3 years	At the age of 5 years
4. Whooping Cough, Tetanus and Diptheria	Triple Antigen	Three times in the 3rd, 4th & 5th month	At the age of $1\frac{1}{2}$ years	At the age of 5 years
5. Polio	Vaccine	Three times in the 3rd, 4th & 5th month	At the age of $1\frac{1}{2}$ years	At the age of 5 years
6. Measles	Vaccine	Between 9 & 13 months	+++	+++
7. Typhoid	Vaccine	At the age of 2 years	One month after the first	Every year before summer
8. Cholera	Vaccine	At the age of 2 years	Every year before summer	In rainy season
9. Eye Trouble	Vitamin 'A'	Every six months—for 5 years		

Points to remember at the time of vaccination

- The child should be absolutely healthy at the time of vaccination.
- If there is any skin trouble, do not have Small-pox vaccination. This vaccination is not given nowadays as it has been totally eradicated.
- If the child had diarrhoea, do not give him polio drops.
- Polio vaccine is more effective in winter than in summer, as its effect may be minimised due to diarrhoea and dysentery.
- Do not breast feed the baby one hour before and after administering polio drops. Bottle feed

HEIGHT AND WEIGHT CHARTS

Age	BOYS			GIRLS		
	Height		Weight kg.	Height		Weight kg.
	Cms.	Ft .		Cms.	Ft.	
Upto 3 months	55.9	1' 10"	4.5	55.9	1' 10"	4.2
4 - 6 "	63.5	2' 1"	6.7	60.9	2' 0"	5.6
7 - 9 "	66.0	2' 2"	6.9	66.0	2' 2"	6.2
10 - 12 "	71.1	2' 4"	7.4	71.1	2' 4"	6.6
1 year	73.7	2' 5"	8.4	73.7	2' 5"	7.8
2 years	81.3	2' 8"	10.1	81.3	2' 8"	9.6
3 "	88.9	2' 11"	11.8	88.9	2' 11"	11.2
4 "	96.5	3' 2"	13.5	96.5	3' 2"	12.9
5 "	104.1	3' 5"	14.8	101.6	3' 4"	14.5
6 "	109.2	3' 7"	16.3	109.2	3' 7"	16.0
7 "	114.3	3' 9"	18.0	114.3	3' 9"	17.6
8 "	121.9	4' 0"	19.7	118.2	3' 11"	19.4
9 "	124.5	4' 1"	21.3	124.5	4' 1"	21.3
10 "	129.5	4' 3"	23.5	129.5	4' 3"	23.6
11 "	134.6	4' 5"	25.9	134.6	4' 5"	26.4
12 "	139.7	4' 7"	28.5	139.7	4' 7"	29.8
13 "	147.3	4' 10"	32.1	144.8	4' 9"	33.3
14 "	152.4	5' 0"	35.7	149.9	4' 11"	36.8
15 "	157.5	5' 2"	39.6	152.4	5' 0"	36.8
16 "	162.6	5' 4"	43.2	153.7	5' 1/2"	41.1
17 "	165.1	5' 5"	45.7	153.7	5' 1/2"	42.4

Interesting facts :

1. At 9 years of age, an average healthy boy will be 3/4 (three quarters) of his full adult height.

2. At 18 years of age, the boy will be twice the height he was at 2 years of age.

Interesting facts :

1. At 7 1/2 years of age, an average healthy girl will be 3/4 (three quarters) of her adult height.

2. At 18 years of age, the girl will be twice the height she was at 18 months of age.

SOME TIPS TO CHECK ADULTERATION IN FOODSTUFFS

S.No.	Food item	Adulterated with	Tests
1.	Asafoetida	Sand, gum pebbles	Pure asafoetida will mix well in water and become whitey. When burnt, it will burn vigourously. Adulterated one changes the colour of the water to light yellow.
2.	Black peppercorns	Papaya seeds	When mixed in water, papaya seeds will float, while the peppercorns will settle at the bottom. When powdered, papaya seeds will be ground to a fine powder while peppercorns will remain coarsely powdered.
3.	Black salt	Coal pieces	When mixed with water, salt will dissolve while adulterated material will remain undissolved.
4.	Cinnamon	Dyed bark of different trees	When mixed in a glass of water, the dye would be dissolved in it.
5.	Coffee	Starch, Roasted bread crumbs, powdered date seeds	Prepare some black coffee, add a few drops of sulphuric acid and two drops of tincture iodine. If the mixture turns blue, coffee is adulterated with starch. In case of adulteration by other items, drop a spoonful of coffee in water. Do not stir. Coffee will float for some time while adulterated coffee will go down instantly.
6.	Cumin seeds	Coloured seeds of grass	Press a few seeds of jeera between your fingers. If your fingers get dyed, the food item is adulterated.
7.	Edible oil	Argemone oil, castor oil, mineral oil	If the oil turns red or brown on addition of nitric acid, the oil is adulterated with argemone oil. In case of castor oil adulteration, add petroleum ether, crushed ice and salt into the vessel containing the oil. The mixture will turn sandy brown. In case of mineral oil adulteration, add 1 teaspoon N/2 nitric acid (to 1l water add 2 ml nitric acid) to a teaspoon oil. Boil water in a vessel and dip the test tube containing the mixture into it.

S.No.	Food item	Adulterated with	Tests
8.	Ghee/Butter	Vanaspati ghee or starch	Add equal quantities of melted ghee or butter and hydrochloric acid and pour it into a test tube and shake. If the layer of acid turns pink, the product is adulterated with vanaspati ghee. If the melted ghee/butter turns purple on the addition of tincture iodine, the food item is mixed with starch.
9.	Honey	Glucose	Drop some honey in a glass of water. If the honey is pure, it will settle at the bottom, or else it will dissolve.
10.	Milk/Curd	Water/starch	Put a drop of milk on some flat surface. If the drops stays or leaves a white trail if it flows, the milk is pure. If the milk/curd turns purple on the addition of tincture iodine, the milk is adulterated with starch.
11.	Red chilli (whole) and powder	Inferior quality wood scraps, red colour	Inferior quality red chilli are dyed and sold. To test, rub against the dry chilli with a swab of cotton dipped in oil. If the cotton has traces of red colour, the chillies are dyed. Mix a spoon of red chilli powder in a glass of water. The wood scraps will float. If the water turns red, then red colour has been added.
12.	Sugar	Metal scraps, white sand, sand	Use a magnet to detect metal scraps. In case of other adulterants, add a spoonful of sugar into a glass of water. Sugar will dissolve, but the others will not.
13.	Sweets	Aluminium foil instead of silver foil	Add a few drops of hydrochloric acid on the foil. If it becomes effervescent, aluminium foil is used.
14.	Tea	Coloured tea, iron scraps/ wood scraps	Take a wet blotting paper and spread some tea leaves over it. Remove the tea leaves after some time. If stains are left behind, the tea has been used and then dyed. To detect iron scraps, use a magnet. Mix some tea leaves in water, wood scraps will float on water.

Rapidex
Home Management Guide

—*Rupa Chatierjee*

A well-managed Home is a mirror of a good housewife's personality.

- **Interior Decoration • Time Management • Housekeeping**
- **Kitchen Management • Health & Hygiene • Budget Management**
- **Etiquette & Manners • Personality Grooming • Family Relations**
  ...and anything in your home that needs to be managed.

A housewife is very often judged by the way she keeps her house. For her it's like a temple —a key through which she can ensure highest level of physical and emotional comfort for her family.

And in view of its critical significance in one's life, it's imperative that your home is managed well —an art every homemaker needs to master.

Rapidex Home Management Guide, written by a seasoned housewife who is also a professional interior designer, is one such handy help that deals with the subject in a critical and comprehensive manner. Never before so many tips and suggestions, covering every aspect of the subject, have been put together in a single volume. From interior decoration, time management, organising household chores, cleaning of house and its security, maintaining of gadgets and household articles to household budget, etiquette for all occasions, first aid, travel and transfer, personal grooming, gardening, it goes on to cover tips on energy conservation and interpersonal relationship.

A must for all who wish to make their home a paradise.

Big Size • Pages: 296
Price: Rs. 150/- • Postage: Rs. 20/-

Over 400 Beauty Solutions

...From Tip to Toe

—Tanushree Podder

There is a lot of ignorance and confusion regarding the basic information about beauty. The book addresses the need for information in that field. It proposes to create awareness and knowledge about the subject. It is meant for every questioning mind and for every person who wants to be beautiful.

Big size • Pages: 152
Price: Rs. 96/- • Postage: Rs. 15/-

Reveal your Glow

—Donna Rae

...Brush your body beautiful

The four steps outlined in this book will give you a quantum leap toward better health and beauty of your skin with simple brush, rinse, buff and rub system. *You will:*

• Get younger-looking radiant skin • Stop premature aging • Increase your circulation • Save time and money!

Start and have positive effects on your body, mind and spirit.

Demy size, Pages: 124
Price: Rs. 60/- • Postage: Rs. 10/-

Body & Beauty Care

—*Neena Khanna*

The image a person projects is of basic and significant importance in career development, opportunity, peer status and ultimate achievement.

The importance of beauty in human affairs has long been appreciated by poets and artists. Today much can be done with sophisticated cosmetics to enhance the appearance of an individual.

Body & Beauty Care is primarily intended for the new conscious generation of men and women who groom to look good.

Starting with a basic knowledge of the structures and functioning of the skin, nail, hair and teeth, the book goes on to give the cause and effect of common skin, nail, hair and teeth problems. It provides sound practical advice on the treatment of these problems. A separate chapter deals with the modern trends in cosmetics surgery.

The book is a must for all those who want to look good and feel good about themselves.

Big Size • Pages: 110
Price: Rs. 60/- • Postage: Rs. 10/-

Home Beauty Clinic

—Parvesh Handa

The art of personal beautification by decorative aids is as ancient as human civilization itself. Today much stress is laid on an attractive and impressive personality, which includes the way of talking, walking, dress sense manners, grace and etiquettes.

Although every woman may not have the fairy tale look of Cinderella or the legendary face of a 'Helen of Troy' there is always something particular and charming in every woman. It is, therefore, necessary for her to enhance that intrinsic charm by hiding her natural flaw, if any.

Home Beauty Clinic is an attempt to satisfy the various needs of a beauty-conscious woman, such as facial, massage, make-up, pedicure, manicure, hairstyle etc. This could help make the maintenance of her beauty a routine and every day affair.

The methods of indigenous preparation of cosmetics has been given in detail as they are a safeguard against any side-effects.

Big Size • Pages: 128
Price: Rs. 48/- • Postage: Rs. 10/-

Herbal Beauty Care

—*Rashmi Sharma*

In today's world, every woman has the desire to look beautiful. It has often been thought that well-groomed persons are generally more interesting, strong, poised, outgoing and exciting than poorly groomed individuals.

Today much can be done with sophisticated cosmetics to enhance the appearance of an individual. Cosmetics contribute not only to the appearance but also to health in the fullest sense of skin, psychologic and social wholesomeness.

However, cosmetics harm the skin after prolonged use, hence people are now switching their allegiance to herbal products from synthetic products.

Herbal Beauty Care provides you with:

- ❖ Cosmetic-free easy and effective herbal remedies.
- ❖ Massages and exercises to tone your body.
- ❖ Balanced diet charts.

Big Size • Pages: 144
Price: Rs. 75/- • Postage: Rs. 15/-   (Also available in Hindi)

Reversing Aging

—Dr. Bruce Goldberg

Aging slowly allows us to enjoy life to the hilt, rather than expend our energies resisting Father Time. The very thought of growing old and the inevitable difficulties usually associated with aging depresses most people. Now science is on the threshold of showing us how aging can be prevented, or at least delayed.

Reversing Aging presents both theory and specific techniques to deal with life's challenges associated with aging. The author, Dr. Bruce Goldberg, has drawn the most accurate and useful information available from the fields of personal grooming, gerontology (the study of aging), nutrition, exercise, biochemistry and alternative medicine to help improve and retain your vigour throughout life.

In the book, you will discover:

❖ How to use self-hypnosis to slow down the aging process.

❖ How to take a balanced diet for a longer life.

❖ How to change your lifestyle to preserve youth.

❖ How to change aging indicators.

❖ How to look younger through simple, natural methods.

Demy Size • Pages: 216
Price: Rs. 80/- • Postage: Rs. 15/-
